Key Stage 3 Science

Spectrum 7

Andy Cooke

Jean Martin

CAMBRIDGE
UNIVERSITY PRESS

Series editors	Andy Cooke
	Jean Martin
Authors	Derek Baron
	Trevor Bavage
	Paul Butler
	Andy Cooke
	Zoe Crompton
	Sam Ellis
	Kevin Frobisher
	Jean Martin
	Mick Mulligan
	Chris Ram

PUBLISHED BY THE PRESS SYNDICATE OF THE UNIVERSITY OF CAMBRIDGE
The Pitt Building, Trumpington Street, Cambridge, United Kingdom

CAMBRIDGE UNIVERSITY PRESS
The Edinburgh Building, Cambridge CB2 2RU, UK
40 West 20th Street, New York, NY 10011-4211, USA
477 Williamstown Road, Port Melbourne, VIC 3207, Australia
Ruiz de Alarcón 13, 28014 Madrid, Spain
Dock House, The Waterfront, Cape Town 8001, South Africa

http://www.cambridge.org

First published 2002

Printed in the United Kingdom by Cambridge University Press

Typeface Delima MT   *System* QuarkXPress ®

A catalogue record for this book is available from the British Library

ISBN 0 521 75004 0   paperback

Cover design by Blue Pig Design Co

CONTENTS

About Spectrum

This *Spectrum* Class Book covers what you will learn about science and scientists in Year 7. It is split into twelve **Units**. Each Unit starts with a page like this:

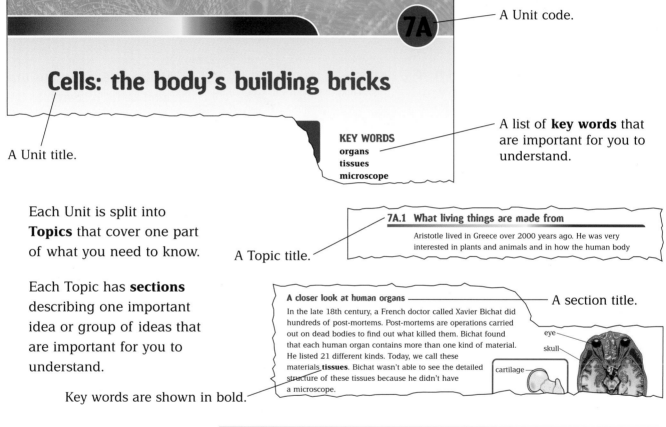

A Unit code.

Cells: the body's building bricks

A Unit title.

KEY WORDS
organs
tissues
microscope

A list of **key words** that are important for you to understand.

Each Unit is split into **Topics** that cover one part of what you need to know.

A Topic title.

7A.1 What living things are made from

Aristotle lived in Greece over 2000 years ago. He was very interested in plants and animals and in how the human body

Each Topic has **sections** describing one important idea or group of ideas that are important for you to understand.

Key words are shown in bold.

A closer look at human organs

In the late 18th century, a French doctor called Xavier Bichat did hundreds of post-mortems. Post-mortems are operations carried out on dead bodies to find out what killed them. Bichat found that each human organ contains more than one kind of material. He listed 21 different kinds. Today, we call these materials **tissues**. Bichat wasn't able to see the detailed structure of these tissues because he didn't have a microscope.

A section title.

eye
skull
cartilage

Each Unit finishes with a **summary** of key words and ideas so you can see what you have learnt.

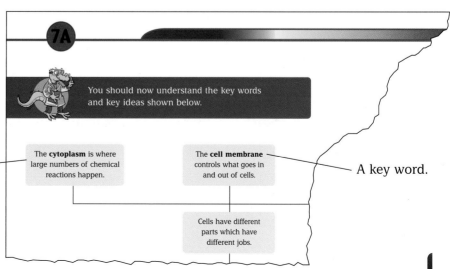

7A

You should now understand the key words and key ideas shown below.

An important idea.

The **cytoplasm** is where large numbers of chemical reactions happen.

The **cell membrane** controls what goes in and out of cells.

A key word.

Cells have different parts which have different jobs.

Doctor Croc, Crocodelia and Al

Doctor Croc introduces each Unit.

Doctor Croc also introduces the summary of key words and ideas at the end of each Unit.

Crocodelia asks questions about what you have just learnt.

Crocodelia also tells you where to look in the class book to help with activities.

Al asks questions that help you think about what you have just learnt.

Al also asks questions that might need some research to answer.

At the end of the book

At the end of the book you will find:

- pages 163 to 168 to help you with **scientific investigations**.

- a **glossary/index** to help you look up words and find out their meanings.

Other components of Spectrum.

Your teacher has other components of *Spectrum*:

- a **Teacher file** or **Teacher CD-ROM** full of information for them and lots of activities of different kinds for you. The activities are split into three levels: **support**, **main** and **extension**. Some of the activities are **suitable for homework**;

- an **assessment CD-ROM** with an **analysis tool**. The CD-ROM has **multiple choice tests** to find out what you know before you start a Unit and for you to do during or after a Unit. It also has some end of year **SAT style tests**;

- a set of **Technician Notes** with information about **practical activities**.

Cells: the body's building bricks

In this unit we shall be learning about some cells, tissues and organs in plants and animals.

7A.1 What living things are made from

Aristotle lived in Greece over 2000 years ago. He was very interested in plants and animals and in how the human body works. Look at the drawing by Aristotle of some parts of the human body. We call these parts **organs**. The Greeks weren't the only people interested in how the body works. Old drawings and texts from China and the Middle East also show human organs. Some even show plant organs.

At first, information about organs came from operations and from cutting up dead bodies. Now we can look at X-rays and body scans, too.

1   Write down the names of <u>two</u> organs that you can see on:
   a Aristotle's drawing;
   b the scan.

A closer look at human organs

In the late 18th century, a French doctor called Xavier Bichat did hundreds of post-mortems. Post-mortems are operations carried out on dead bodies to find out what killed them. Bichat found that each human organ contains more than one kind of material. He listed 21 different kinds. Today, we call these materials **tissues**. Bichat wasn't able to see the detailed structure of these tissues because he didn't have a microscope.

2   Look at this picture of part of a thigh bone. Write down the names of <u>three</u> tissues in this bone.

3   What do we use to see what the cells in these tissues are like?

Cystis (bladder)

Aidoion (penis)

Orchis (testis)

Aristotle's drawing. The names in brackets are the ones that we use.

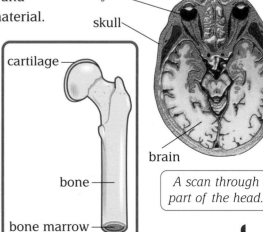

eye

skull

cartilage

brain

bone

bone marrow

A scan through part of the head.

Part of a thigh bone.

7A.2 How microscopes helped to change our ideas

Microscopes were invented in the 16th century. The lenses of these microscopes were not very good, so the images were not clear. The first microscopes had only one lens. They were called simple microscopes.

It was not until 1590 that two Dutch spectacle makers, Hans and Zacharias Janssen, made a microscope with two lenses. We call this kind a <u>compound</u> microscope.

Later, an English scientist called Robert Hooke built a compound microscope. He used it to look at things that were too small to see with the naked eye. In 1665, he published the first book of drawings of these microscopic structures. One of the drawings was of a slice of cork.

Cork is the bark of a cork oak tree. Hooke's microscope showed that cork is made up of what look like tiny boxes. Hooke called these boxes **cells**.

In 1673, a Dutchman called Antonie van Leeuwenhoek found out how to make better lenses. He made a simple microscope with one of these lenses. His microscope made things look 200 times bigger than they really were. We say that it magnified things 200 times. Because his lens was so much better, the images were clearer than Hooke's. Leeuwenhoek published a book of drawings of microscopic creatures in 1683.

About 150 years later, a Scot called Robert Brown saw that there was something inside cells. He named this the **nucleus** in 1831.

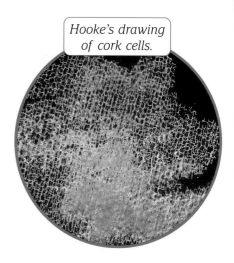
Hooke's drawing of cork cells.

Leeuwenhoek's microscope

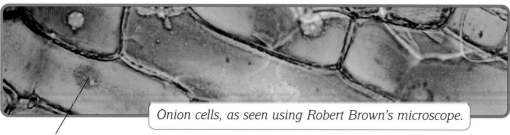
Onion cells, as seen using Robert Brown's microscope.

nucleus

By 1840, two German scientists called Matthias Schleiden and Theodor Schwann realised that all plants and animals were made of cells. They published this idea as a theory, called simply <u>cell theory</u>.

1 In one sentence, write down what you think that cell theory says.

2 Use the information on this page to draw a time-line for the invention of lenses and the microscope and the discovery of cells.

Scale drawings

When we draw what we see under a microscope, we draw things much bigger than they really are. We draw them to **scale**. We often use scale drawings in our lives, not just in science. Maps and plans are scale diagrams. They show places smaller than they really are. We call this <u>scaling down</u>. When we show things bigger than they really are, we are <u>scaling up</u>. You can show a scale in one of these ways:

× 20

1 mm

3 a Why did Hooke draw the flea larger than life?

b Is this scaling up or scaling down?

c Adding a scale would make Hooke's drawing more useful. Explain why.

4 a How long is the ladybird in Leon's drawing?

b How many times longer is the drawing than the real ladybird?

c What is the scale factor of the drawing?

5 Draw the ladybird magnified 20 times. Remember to put a scale on your drawing.

6 Think about <u>two</u> jobs in which people draw things to scale. Explain why they need to use scale drawings.

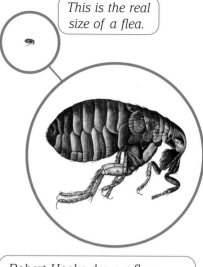
This is the real size of a flea.

Robert Hooke drew a flea bigger than it really is. This means you can see more detail.

This ladybird is 4 mm long.

Under a magnifying lens the ladybird looks three times as big, so the scale factor is ×3.

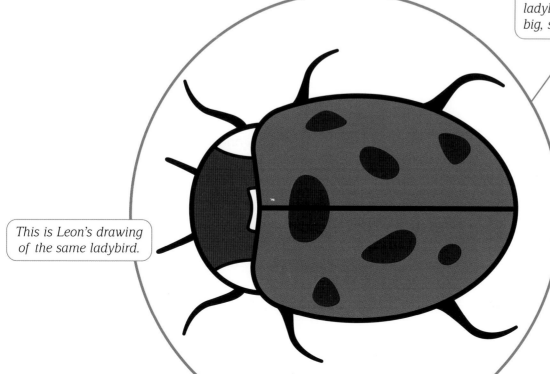
This is Leon's drawing of the same ladybird.

7A.3 What cells are like

Cells are very small

Remember that all living things are made of cells and that cells are so small that you need a microscope to see them. If you magnify cells a hundred times or more, you can see the smaller parts inside them. Not everything has got this type of detail. Many non-living things show no structure when you look at them under a microscope.

1 Look at the photos of thin layers from a candle and skin from a stick of rhubarb taken through a microscope.

   a What does the microscope view of the candle wax show?

   b What does the microscope view of the stick of rhubarb show?

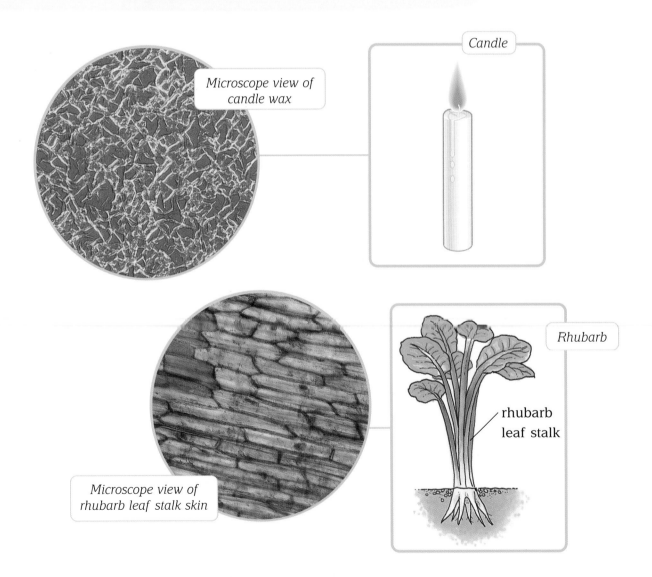

Microscope view of candle wax

Candle

Microscope view of rhubarb leaf stalk skin

Rhubarb

rhubarb leaf stalk

2 Look at the microscope views of living and non-living things. Which ones do you think are of living things? Explain your answers.

Microscope views of living and non-living things.

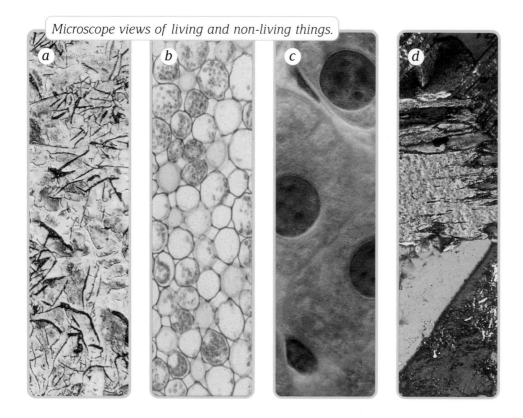

a

b

c

d

Cells are not all alike

All cells are very small, but they are not all the same size. In this square □ you could fit 2500 rhubarb skin cells or 10 000 human skin cells. Cells can be different shapes. Plant and animal cells look quite different under the microscope.

3 Which cells are bigger, rhubarb or human cells?

4 Look at the diagrams below. Describe <u>two</u> differences between the plant and animal cells.

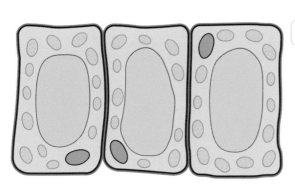

Plant cells

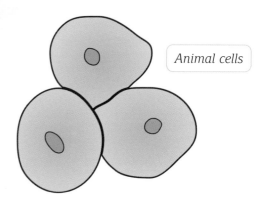

Animal cells

A closer look at animal cells

Cells are made of lots of different parts. Each part has a different job to do to keep the cell alive and working properly. Chris made a slide of some cheek cells. The picture shows what they looked like under the microscope.

5 Which part of a cell controls everything that goes on in the cell?

6 Why do you think a cell membrane is very thin?

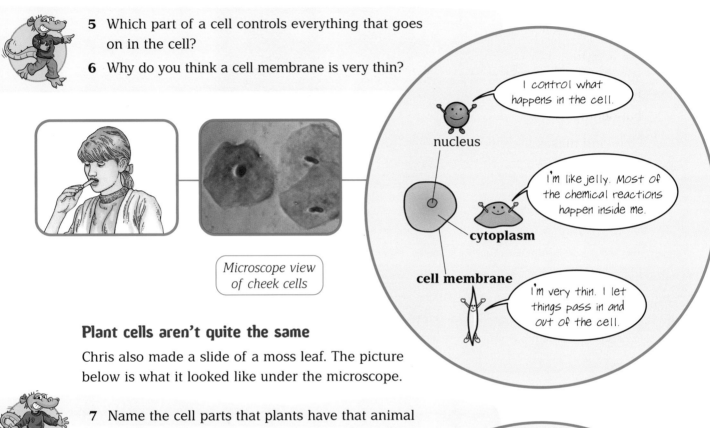

Microscope view of cheek cells

nucleus

I control what happens in the cell.

I'm like jelly. Most of the chemical reactions happen inside me.

cytoplasm

cell membrane

I'm very thin. I let things pass in and out of the cell.

Plant cells aren't quite the same

Chris also made a slide of a moss leaf. The picture below is what it looked like under the microscope.

7 Name the cell parts that plants have that animal cells don't have.

8 Which part controls what happens in a plant cell?

9 The roots of a plant are not green. Which part of a plant cell shown on the diagram is missing from root cells?

10 Write down <u>one</u> difference between these cell parts:

    a a nucleus and a chloroplast;

    b a cell wall and a cell membrane.

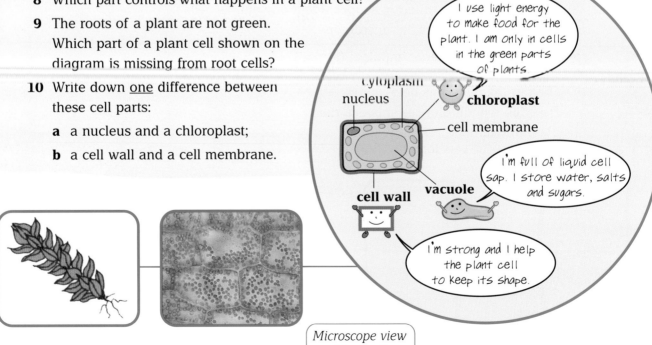

I use light energy to make food for the plant. I am only in cells in the green parts of plants

cytoplasm

nucleus

chloroplast

cell membrane

cell wall

vacuole

I'm full of liquid cell sap. I store water, salts and sugars.

I'm strong and I help the plant cell to keep its shape.

Microscope view of leaf cells

7A.4 Different cells for different jobs

There are over a million different types of animals. They all have different shapes and sizes. But in all these animals there are only about 200 different kinds of cells. These cells are different because of the jobs they do, not because of the kind of animal they are found in.

This page shows some of the cells in animals and plants and the jobs that they do. For example, when you breathe in air you sometimes breathe in dust as well. This dust can clog up your lungs. Two kinds of cells in your breathing tubes stop this happening.

One kind makes the lining sticky with mucus. Dust gets trapped in this mucus. We call these cells <u>goblet cells</u> because of their shape.

The other kind has tiny hairs that carry the mucus and dust out of your lungs. A tissue that forms a skin or a lining is called an epithelial tissue and the hairs are called cilia. So we call these cells <u>ciliated epithelial cells.</u>

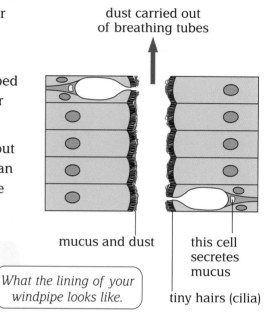

dust carried out of breathing tubes

mucus and dust

this cell secretes mucus

tiny hairs (cilia)

What the lining of your windpipe looks like.

1 How are ciliated epithelial cells different from other animal cells?

When you see, hear, smell, taste or touch anything you are using special cells. These special cells are called <u>nerve cells</u>. Nerve cells are very different from other animal cells because they are very long. They have to carry messages in the form of nerve impulses from one part of your body to another. Your brain and spinal cord can send and receive nerve impulses from all over your body.

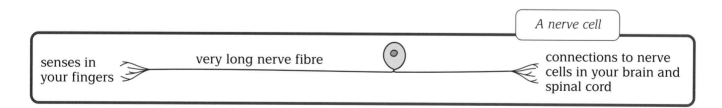

A nerve cell

senses in your fingers

very long nerve fibre

connections to nerve cells in your brain and spinal cord

2 How long is the nerve cell from your fingertip to your spinal cord? Hint: Measure the distance from your backbone to your fingertip.

The cells of your body need oxygen to stay alive. Special cells in your blood carry oxygen around your body. These special cells are called <u>red blood cells</u>. They are full of a chemical called haemoglobin which combines with oxygen. So the cells can carry oxygen to every cell in the body.

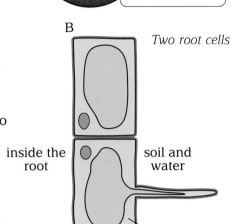

A red blood cell

B

Two root cells

3 The more haemoglobin there is in a red blood cell the more oxygen it can carry. Red blood cells do not have a nucleus. Why do you think this is?

It's not just animals that have special cells. Plants need water to stay alive. They take it in through special cells in their roots. These cells are called <u>root hair cells</u>.

inside the root

soil and water

4 Here are two cells from a root. Why do you think the root hair cell (A) can take in more water than the other root cell (B)?

root hair cell

A

How cells work together

A house does not look like a living thing! However, the way the building materials of a house are grouped is similar to the way that cells in a living thing are organised. The bricks in a house are like the cells in a living thing. A group of bricks is called a wall. A group of similar cells is called a tissue. All the cells in a tissue are the same and work together to do the same job.

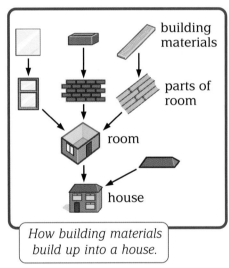

building materials

parts of room

room

house

How building materials build up into a house.

5 Muscle cells work together in muscle tissue. What do you think is the job of muscle tissue?

In a house, different groups of building materials are joined together to make the rooms. In a living thing, several tissues are joined together to make an organ.

There are many different rooms in a house, and each room is needed for a different reason. In a living thing there are many different organs, and each organ has a different job.

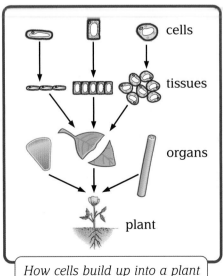

cells

tissues

organs

plant

How cells build up into a plant

6 The leaf of a plant is an organ. It is made of several different tissues. What job does the leaf do?

7 Why is a petal an organ?

8 a Can you think of some rooms in a house that are the same?

b You have more than one of some organs in your body. Write down <u>one</u> example.

7A.5 How new cells are made

People used to think that living things sometimes appeared out of nowhere. They saw for themselves that maggots appeared in rotting meat, and Leeuwenhoek described tiny living animals in rotting things. So the idea seemed to be sensible. In the 19th century Louis Pasteur proved that this idea was wrong. He showed that living things come only from other living things.

Cells are the building blocks of life, and they don't just appear from nowhere either. In 1858, a German scientist called Rudolph Virchow suggested that new cells could only grow from cells that were already there. Now we know that new cells form only when existing cells divide.

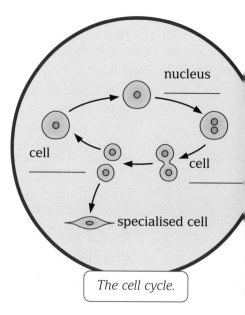

The cell cycle.

How a cell divides

The nucleus divides first, then the cell. As the new cells take in more materials, they grow. When they are big enough, the cells divide again. We call this the cell cycle.

1 Make a copy of the cell cycle diagram.
Complete the labels on your copy.

When a plant cell divides, a new wall forms between the new nuclei. Some cells divide over and over again, but other cells become specialised to do particular jobs. Specialised cells don't divide again.

2 Think of <u>one</u> reason why a specialised cell can't divide.

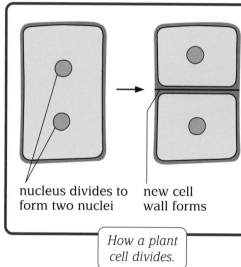

nucleus divides to form two nuclei   new cell wall forms

How a plant cell divides.

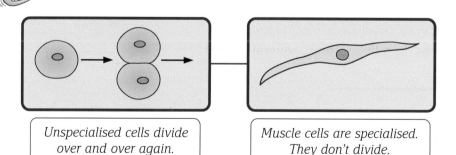

Unspecialised cells divide over and over again.

Muscle cells are specialised. They don't divide.

The nucleus controls how a cell develops

The nucleus of a cell holds all the information that tells a cell how to work and develop. Before it divides, the nucleus makes a copy of this information. One copy goes into each new nucleus. So the new cells are identical to the old ones.

3 Describe how information passes to new cells.

7A.6 The secret life of plants

A flower is the reproductive system of a plant. Its job is to make seeds which can grow into new plants. The flower has special sex cells to make seeds. Pollen contains the male sex cell, and the ovule contains the female sex cell. The pollen must travel from the male part of a plant to the female part of the same plant, or of another plant of the same kind.

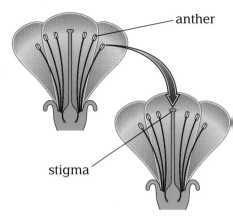

1   How do you think pollen gets from one flower to another?

2   Pollen contains the male sex cell of plants.
    What is the male sex cell of humans called?

Pollen travels from an anther to a stigma. This is called pollination.

Once the pollen has reached the female part of a plant, the pollen grows a tube down to the ovule. The nucleus of the male sex cell travels down this tube to join with the nucleus of the ovule. Each nucleus contains half of the information to pass on to the new plant. When the two nuclei fuse, they make one complete nucleus in the first cell of the new plant. This first cell then grows and divides to make a seed.

3   Why does pollen need to grow a tube once it has landed on the stigma of a flower?

Growing pollen tubes

A pollen grain is very small. The male sex cell is inside. The outer wall of a pollen grain is strong, and in some plants it is spiky.

4   Why do you think some pollen grains are covered in spikes?

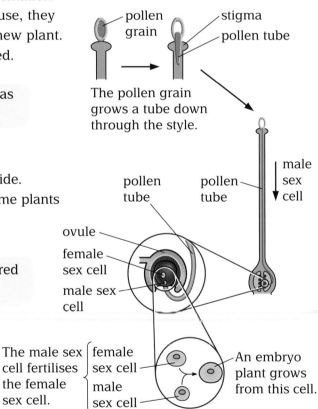

The pollen grain grows a tube down through the style.

The male sex cell fertilises the female sex cell.

Pollen tube growth and fertilisation

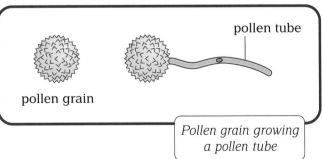

pollen tube

pollen grain

Pollen grain growing a pollen tube

A pollen tube grows when a pollen grain sticks to the stigma of a flower and the nucleus of the male sex cell travels down this tube to reach the female sex cell. Sometimes it is possible to get pollen tubes to grow in sugary water.

Yasmin decided to do an experiment to grow pollen tubes. Look at the pictures to see what she did.

5 Look at the microscope slide. How many pollen tubes grew?

Yasmin tried the same experiment with pollen from a different flower. This time she used nasturtiums. She did not manage to get any pollen tubes to grow. She thought that the problem could be the concentration of the sugary water. She decided to investigate if the concentration of the sugary water affects how many pollen tubes grow.

6 Write a list of all the things that Yasmin needed to keep the same to make this a fair test.

7 Yasmin decided to make two slides for each sugar concentration. Why was this a good idea?

Yasmin collected some pollen grains from chickweed. She used a paintbrush to carefully pick up the pollen grains from a flower.

Next Yasmin put the pollen grains onto a microscope slide. Then she added a drop of sugary water to the slide. She left the slide in the dark for two hours.

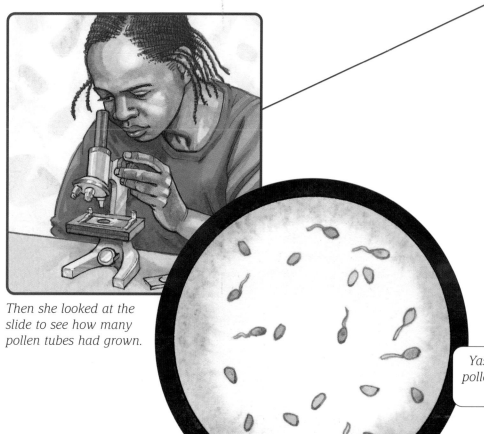

Then she looked at the slide to see how many pollen tubes had grown.

Yasmin's view of the pollen grains down the microscope.

You should now understand the key words and key ideas shown below.

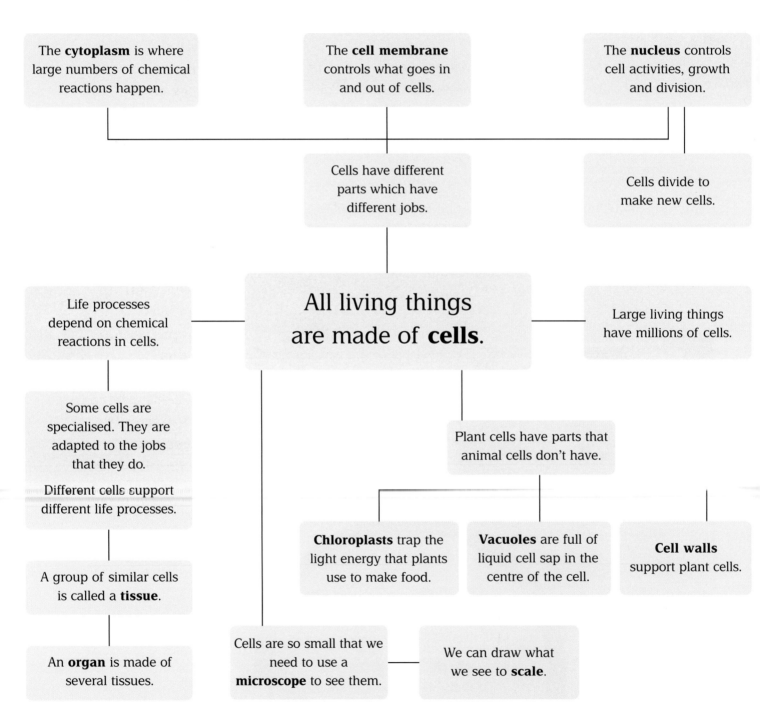

The **cytoplasm** is where large numbers of chemical reactions happen.

The **cell membrane** controls what goes in and out of cells.

The **nucleus** controls cell activities, growth and division.

Cells have different parts which have different jobs.

Cells divide to make new cells.

Life processes depend on chemical reactions in cells.

All living things are made of **cells**.

Large living things have millions of cells.

Some cells are specialised. They are adapted to the jobs that they do.

Different cells support different life processes.

Plant cells have parts that animal cells don't have.

A group of similar cells is called a **tissue**.

Chloroplasts trap the light energy that plants use to make food.

Vacuoles are full of liquid cell sap in the centre of the cell.

Cell walls support plant cells.

An **organ** is made of several tissues.

Cells are so small that we need to use a **microscope** to see them.

We can draw what we see to **scale**.

Reproduction

In this unit we shall be learning about reproduction and some of the different ways that humans and other animals make sure that their kind continues to exist.

KEY WORDS
reproduce
sex cells
sperm
egg cell
fuse
fertilisation
uterus
testis
ovary
oviduct
ovulation
embryo
implantation
fetus
inherits
menstrual cycle
menstruation
placenta
amniotic fluid
mammary glands
adolescence
puberty
**secondary sexual
  characteristics**

7B.1 How a new life starts

All animals die. So they must produce young. They **reproduce** so that their kind survives.

In many animals, a new life starts when the nuclei of two **sex cells** join. One of these sex cells comes from the mother. The other sex cell comes from the father. We call this kind of reproduction <u>sexual reproduction</u>.

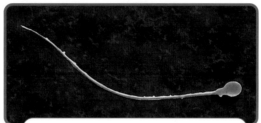

*A male sex cell. We call it a **sperm**. A sperm swims to reach an egg cell.*

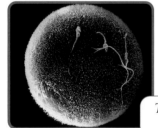

*This female sex cell, or **egg cell**, is much bigger than the sperm cells around it.*

tail for swimming

nuclei of sperm and egg cell joined together

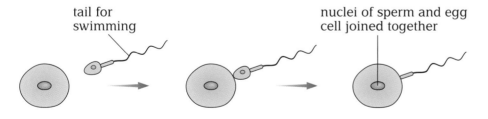

*A new life starts when the nucleus of a sperm joins with the nucleus of an egg cell. We say that the nuclei **fuse**. This fusing is called **fertilisation**.*

1 What do we call male sex cells?

2 What do we call female sex cells?

3 A sperm is a specialised cell. What special feature helps it to reach the egg cell?

4 What is fertilisation?

Patterns of reproduction

Different animals fertilise their eggs in different ways. Male fish and male frogs fertilise the egg cells outside the female's body. We call this <u>external</u> fertilisation. The egg cells of birds and mammals are fertilised inside the female's body. We call this <u>internal</u> fertilisation.

Look at the pictures. The eggs of fish and frogs don't have shells. They would dry up if they were laid on land, so they are laid in water. Each egg contains only a little stored food.

Penguins are birds. They lay one or two eggs. Each egg contains lots of stored food.

Most fish and frogs don't look after their eggs and young. They need to lay lots of eggs to make sure that a few survive.

Penguins look after their eggs and young.

Mammals are different again. Their young grow in a special organ inside the mother's body. We call this organ the **uterus**. After they are born, one or both parents feed and protect their young until they can look after themselves.

5 Shells protect the eggs of birds and reptiles. Write down <u>two</u> things that shells protect eggs against.

6 A large female fish like a cod can lay up to 7 million eggs. Explain, as fully as you can, why she needs to lay so many.

7 Each cod egg contains only a little stored food. Why do you think this is?

8 In some animals the eggs are fertilised inside the female. Why does this happen in:

   a birds;   **b** mammals?

9 The eggs of mammals have a good chance of developing and growing up. Eggs laid in water or on land have a smaller chance. Why is this?

Cats look after their young until they are old enough to find their own food and protect themselves.

Reproduction in humans

Humans are mammals. So:

- human eggs have no shell;
- fertilisation happens inside the mother's body;
- the young develop in the mother's uterus;`
- after they are born, the young feed on milk;
- one or both parents look after the young. Often other adults and older children help too.

Look at the diagrams.

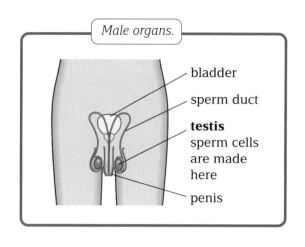

Male organs.

bladder
sperm duct
testis
sperm cells are made here
penis

10 Write down the name of the organ that makes:

  a sperm;

  b egg cells.

A woman releases an egg cell from one of her ovaries about once a month. This is called **ovulation**. Fertilisation can happen only as the egg cell travels down an oviduct. When sperm cells meet an egg cell, the sperm make a special chemical to break down the outer part of the egg cell. Then the nucleus of <u>one</u> sperm can join with the nucleus of the egg cell. We say that the egg cell is fertilised when this happens.

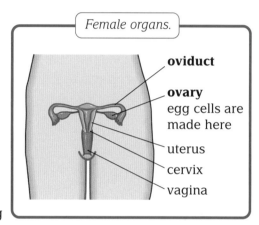

Female organs.

oviduct
ovary
egg cells are made here
uterus
cervix
vagina

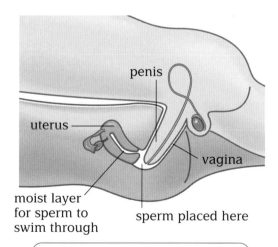

penis

uterus

vagina

moist layer for sperm to swim through

sperm placed here

Over 200 million sperm cells travel from the testes through the penis and into the vagina.

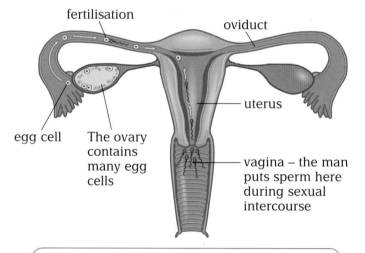

fertilisation

oviduct

uterus

egg cell

The ovary contains many egg cells

vagina – the man puts sperm here during sexual intercourse

Note that the sperm and egg cells are really much smaller than the diagram shows. An egg cell is the size of a tiny speck of sand. You need a microscope to see sperm.

11 Where does fertilisation happen?

12 Write down a list of the parts that a sperm cell passes through on its way from the testis to the egg cell.

13 How do the sperm get from the vagina into an oviduct?

From fertilised egg to baby

Once the egg cell has been fertilised, it grows and divides as it travels down the oviduct into the uterus. First it forms two cells, then four cells, then eight cells. By the time it reaches the uterus, it is a whole ball of cells called an **embryo**.

The lining of the uterus is thick, with lots of blood vessels. The embryo settles into the lining. This is called **implantation**. Now the mother's blood can supply the embryo with the food and oxygen that it needs to grow.

14 How long does it take for the ball of cells to reach the uterus?

15 What is implantation? Why is implantation important?

16 Before all its main organs have started to grow, we call the developing baby an embryo. Later, it looks like a baby but its organs are not fully developed. What do we call it then?

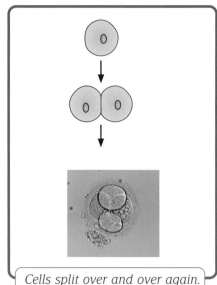

Cells split over and over again.

Growth of the embryo, fetus and baby after implantation. The pictures are not to scale.

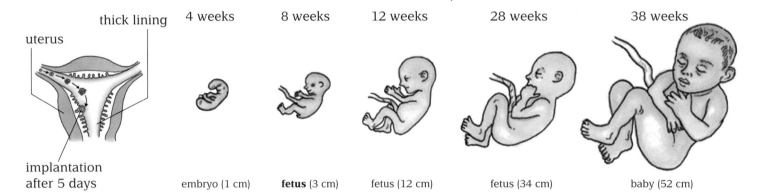

Time since fertilisation

uterus — thick lining — 4 weeks — 8 weeks — 12 weeks — 28 weeks — 38 weeks

implantation after 5 days — embryo (1 cm) — **fetus** (3 cm) — fetus (12 cm) — fetus (34 cm) — baby (52 cm)

Why children are like their parents

The nuclei of the sex cells contain the pattern for a new life. So, the fertilised egg cell **inherits** part of the pattern from each parent. That is why parents, a child and its brothers and sisters have some features in common.

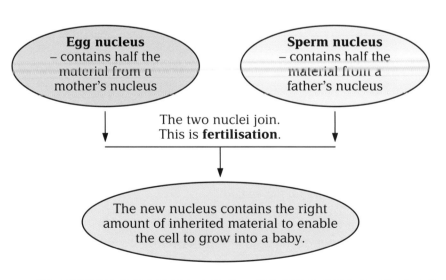

Egg nucleus – contains half the material from a mother's nucleus

Sperm nucleus – contains half the material from a father's nucleus

The two nuclei join. This is **fertilisation**.

The new nucleus contains the right amount of inherited material to enable the cell to grow into a baby.

Half of the inherited material came from the mother and half from the father, so the baby will have some features from each parent.

Some brothers and sisters are more alike than others

Twins are born at the same time. They can be identical or non-identical.

The twins in the first picture grew after two egg cells were fertilised by two different sperm. They inherited some of the same features from their parents, but they also inherited some features that are not the same. So, they are <u>non-identical</u> twins.

The twins in the second picture grew after one fertilised egg cell divided to form two separate embryos. They inherited the same pattern from their parents, so they are <u>identical</u> twins.

Non-identical twins

Identical twins

17 How much of the inherited material in the nucleus of a fertilised egg cell comes from the father?

18 Copy and complete the diagram below.

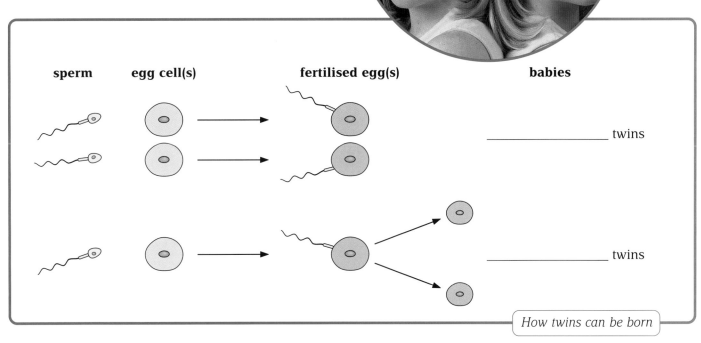

sperm	egg cell(s)	fertilised egg(s)	babies

_____ twins

_____ twins

How twins can be born

19 Are non-identical twins more alike than any other brothers and sisters? Explain your answer.

7B.2 The menstrual cycle

To survive and grow, an embryo has to be implanted in the lining of the uterus. For this to happen, the uterus lining must be ready for it. Timing is important. There is a cycle that links the release of an ovum (egg cell) to the development of the uterus lining. This cycle is called the **menstrual cycle**.
Each menstrual cycle lasts about a month.

1 Why does the lining of the uterus thicken every month?

2 An ovum is released about halfway through the cycle. Explain why this timing is important.

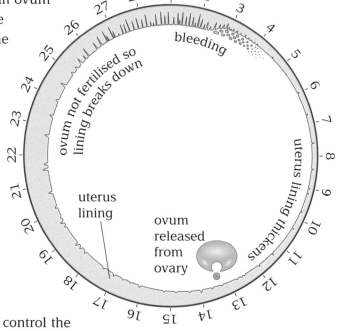

The menstrual cycle. Days are numbered from the first day of bleeding.

Special chemicals called <u>hormones</u> control the menstrual cycle. These chemicals are so powerful they can even change how a woman feels at different times in the cycle.

If an egg is not fertilised, the lining of the uterus breaks down. The woman 'bleeds', or has a 'period'. We call this bleeding **menstruation**.
If an egg is fertilised and an embryo is implanted, the lining does not break down. Menstruation stops.

3 What do we call the time of the month when a woman is bleeding?

4 Where does the blood:

   a come from?

   b leave the woman's body?

5 Why does menstruation stop when a woman is pregnant?

7B.3 The uterus as home to the developing baby

The uterus has a thick muscular wall. As the fetus grows, the wall of the uterus stretches. A special organ called the **placenta** grows in the lining of the uterus.

In the placenta, the blood of the fetus and the blood of the mother are very close but <u>they do not mix</u>. So, substances can pass across the placenta between the blood of the fetus and the blood of the mother.

The fetus needs food and oxygen to grow. These substances pass across the placenta from the mother's blood. The fetus also needs to get rid of waste materials. These pass across the placenta into the mother's blood. The mother's body keeps the fetus at a constant temperature.

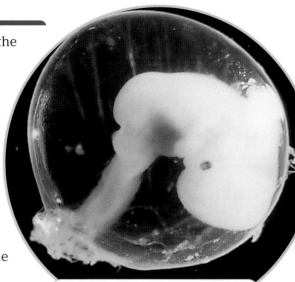

*There is a bag of thin skin around the embryo. This bag is full of a liquid called **amniotic fluid**. This fluid supports the embryo and protects it against shocks.*

1 Look at the pictures. Write down the job of

    a the umbilical cord;

    b the amniotic fluid.

2 Draw a diagram to show <u>two</u> substances passing across the placenta:

    a from the mother to the fetus;

    b from the fetus to the mother.

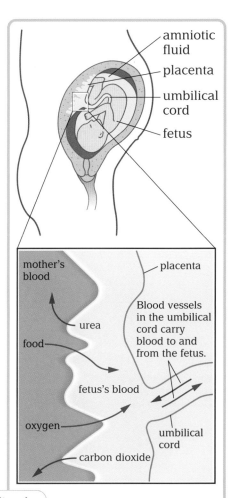

Sadly, harmful substances, such as alcohol and other drugs, can also cross the placenta into the fetus's blood. Some of them can harm the fetus as it grows.

- On average, babies born to mothers who smoke weigh less and have more health problems than babies born to non-smokers.

- A few babies are born addicted to alcohol or other drugs.

- Rubella (German measles) is a virus infection. If a mother gets it in the first three months of pregnancy, her baby may be born deaf and blind.

3 Write down <u>three</u> things that a pregnant woman should be careful to avoid. Explain your answers.

As the embryo grows, it becomes a fetus. The placenta supplies the fetus with food and oxygen and takes away waste materials.

7B.4 Birth and care of the baby

We call childbirth 'labour' because it is hard work. When a baby is born, it passes out of the uterus and through the vagina into the outside world. Before this can happen, a strong muscle around the opening of the uterus must relax and open up. This muscle is part of the cervix. When the baby is ready to be born, many strong contractions of the muscles of the uterus pull the cervix open. Once the cervix is open, the baby's head can go down into the vagina. Then the mother has to use the muscles of her abdomen, too. She has to push hard to get the baby out.

The next job is to make sure that there is no fluid in the baby's nose and mouth, so that it can take its first breath. A short time later, contractions of the uterus push the placenta out, too. We call this the afterbirth.

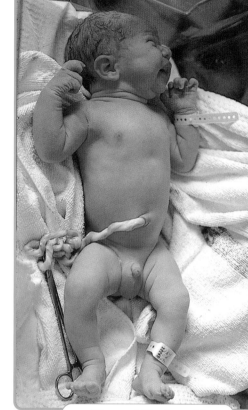

1 Write down <u>two</u> sets of muscles that contract to push the baby out.

2 What is the afterbirth?

3 The umbilical cord is clamped before it is cut. Why do you think the cord is clamped?

The newborn baby is cleaned, checked to make sure that there are no problems and then wrapped up to keep it warm.

The umbilical cord is clamped before it is cut.

Baby care

Looking after a baby is also hard work. Human babies are entirely dependent on their parents and other adults.

Babies need to be kept clean.

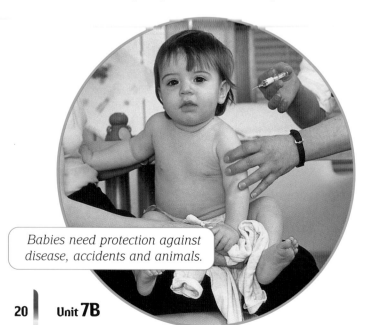

Babies need protection against disease, accidents and animals.

The natural food for young mammals is milk. Milk is made in a mammal's **mammary glands**. The composition of milk is different in different mammals. Many human mothers prefer to feed their babies using their own breast milk. This milk contains substances that destroy some of the micro-organisms that cause infections in humans. So it also helps to protect the baby against these infections.

4 Look at the pie charts. Write down <u>three</u> differences between human milk and cow's milk.

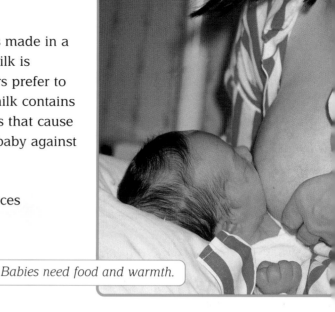

Babies need food and warmth.

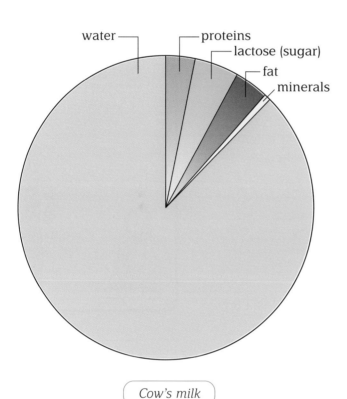

Cow's milk

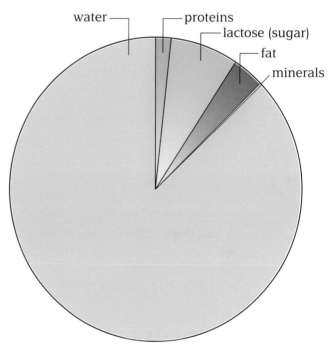

Human milk

5 Milk is sometimes called a 'complete food'. But some things that humans need in their diet are not in milk. Write down <u>one</u> of them.

6 Newborn babies don't control their body temperature. Why do you think this is?

Human children depend on adults for many years. Babies have to learn to control their bodies, to talk and to walk. Usually many adults and older children help to care for them and to teach them. Children also learn many things for themselves.

7B.5 How humans change as they grow

Some children grow up faster than others. But all children grow faster at certain times. Children also change as they grow.

This takes about 9 months.

fertilised egg starts to grow. → embryo → fetus

adult

baby

adolescent ← child

This takes about 20 years.

The human life cycle

1 On a copy of the human life cycle diagram, label:

a the time of birth;

b the two periods between birth and adulthood when a person grows fastest. Use the graph to help you.

2 Write down <u>two</u> differences between the baby and the toddler in the picture.

Sometimes it is difficult to tell whether a young child is a boy or a girl.

Before birth and in the early years, a child's head grows faster than its body. Later, the body grows faster, and boys and girls start to look less alike.

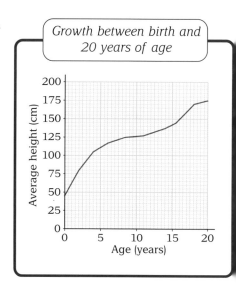

Growth between birth and 20 years of age

Children grow quickly from babies to toddlers.

Young boys and girls have the same body shape.

A time of rapid growth and change starts in the early teens, at anything between nine and 16 years. Often the changes start earlier in girls than in boys. We call the time between childhood and adulthood **adolescence**.

At this time, a gland in the brain starts to make extra hormones. These are special chemicals that make cells grow and divide faster. They also make the testes and ovaries mature and produce sex hormones. At **puberty**, the mature testes and ovaries start to release sex cells.

3   To your diagram for question 1, add:

   a adolescence, the time between chidhood and adulthood;

   b puberty, the time when adolescents become sexually mature.

The testes and ovaries make different hormones. So boys and girls develop in different ways.

Body parts other than the sex organs develop special features. We call these features **secondary sexual characteristics**. When these develop, it becomes easier to tell a boy from a girl.

Other changes during adolescence and puberty	
Girls	**Boys**
Pubic and underarm hair grows.	Pubic and underarm hair grows.
Breasts grow.	Facial and body hair grows.
Ovaries start to release eggs.	Voice deepens.
Monthly periods (of bleeding) begin.	Testes start to make sperm.

4   **a** What are secondary sexual characteristics?

   b Write down <u>two</u> examples of secondary sexual characteristics.

5   Look at the pictures and the table. Write down <u>two</u> changes that happen during adolescence to:

   a both boys and girls;   **b** girls only;   **c** boys only.

Sex hormones also cause emotional changes. So adolescence is often a difficult time, especially as changes take place at different rates in different young people.

6   Why is there no need to worry if you start the changes of adolescence earlier or later than your friends?

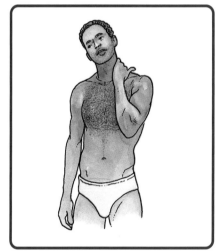

Usually, men have broader chests and shoulders and more muscle than women.

Women develop broader hips and breasts as they grow up.

You should know and understand the key words and key ideas shown below.

Key words

reproduce	uterus	implantation	amniotic fluid
sex cells	testis	fetus	mammary glands
sperm	ovary	inherits	adolescence
egg cell	oviduct	menstrual cycle	puberty
fuse	ovulation	menstruation	secondary sexual characteristics
fertilisation	embryo	placenta	

Key ideas

1. ● Living things produce young of the same kind as themselves. We say that they reproduce.

   ● Different animals reproduce in different ways.

2. ● In sexual reproduction, the nuclei of a sperm and an egg cell join, or fuse. We call this fertilisation.

   ● Sperm and egg cells are specialised to do their jobs.

   ● Sperm and egg nuclei contain inherited material from the parent that made them.

3. ● Women have a monthly cycle controlled by hormones. We call it the menstrual cycle. An egg cell is released and menstruation happens about once a month as part of this cycle.

   ● The menstrual cycle stops when a woman becomes pregnant.

4. ● A fertilised egg cell divides and grows to form an embryo. It is implanted in the uterus.

   ● When the embryo has grown all its main organs, we call it a fetus. The placenta supplies the needs of the fetus through the umbilical cord, and the amniotic fluid cushions it.

5. ● After it is born, mammary glands (breasts) produce milk for the baby.

   ● Human children are dependent on their parents and other adults for a long time.

6. ● The time between childhood and adulthood is called adolescence. Hormones control the changes that take place during this time.

   ● We call the time of sexual maturity puberty. This is when eggs and sperm are first released.

Environment and feeding relationships

In this unit we shall be learning how plants and animals are adapted to the places in which they live and to daily and seasonal change. We shall then study feeding relationships, including food chains and webs.

KEY WORDS
habitats
adapted
environmental
   conditions
nocturnal
seasons
climatic
   stresses
migrate
hibernation
camouflage
producers
herbivores
carnivores
predators
prey
food chains
consumers
food webs
compete

7C.1 Habitats

Habitats are places where plants and animals live. Your body is a habitat. Your skin is home to as many micro-organisms as there are people on Earth!
Sometimes fleas, lice, flatworms and roundworms make their homes in or on your body.

A pond is a habitat with:

- fresh (not salty) water;
- a small temperature range;
- less light as you go deeper;
- less oxygen as you go deeper;
- a variety of food sources.

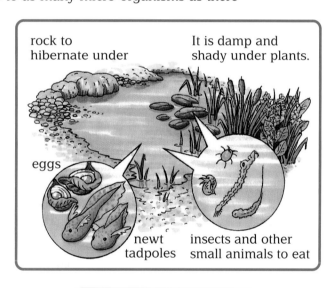

rock to hibernate under

It is damp and shady under plants.

eggs

newt tadpoles

insects and other small animals to eat

A pond is a watery habitat.

A plant or animal's habitat provides the right conditions for it to survive. Each plant or animal has features that suit it to the conditions. We say that the plant or animal is **adapted** to these **environmental conditions**.

Look at the pictures of the newt tadpoles and the newt. The tadpoles are smaller than the adult newt, with no legs and with gills instead of lungs. They spend all their time in the water.

A great crested newt

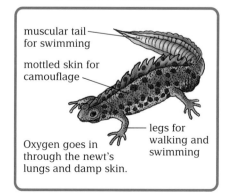

muscular tail for swimming

mottled skin for camouflage

Oxygen goes in through the newt's lungs and damp skin.

legs for walking and swimming

1   Draw a large copy of one newt tadpole. Label the ways that the tadpole is adapted to its habitat (to help you, look at the way the adult newt is labelled).

Plants need light to make food, so their leaves need to be near or above the surface of the water.

2 Look at the drawing. Explain how the duckweed and the water lily get enough light to grow.

Environmental conditions, such as the amount of light or water, are different in different habitats. So different habitats support different plants and animals.

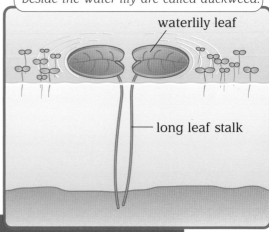

The tiny plants floating on the water beside the water lily are called duckweed.

waterlily leaf

long leaf stalk

Two land habitats	
Grassland	**Woodland**
Plenty of light	Trees shade the ground
Fairly large range of temperatures	Smaller range of temperatures
Exposed to the wind	Sheltered from the wind
Fairly dry soil	Damper soil
Less humid air	More humid air

Some animals shelter among plants, while others burrow in the soil	Animals live in trees and other plants, in leaf litter and in burrows

Some adaptations for burrowing are:

● a cylindrical or streamlined shape;

● strong legs and clawed feet;

● good senses of smell and vibration (although often the sense of sight is poor in these animals).

3 List the adaptations for burrowing of:

a the earthworm;

b the mole.

An earthworm has a long, thin body and slimy skin.

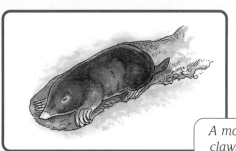

A mole has strong claws for digging.

4 Rabbits also burrow, but their legs are longer than those of moles and they see well to the front and side. Explain how longer legs and good eyesight help rabbits to survive.

5 The thrush can fly and has good eyesight. It sees in colour and is a good judge of distance. Its speckled feathers are good camouflage. These are useful adaptations for living in woodlands. Explain why.

A song thrush

7C.2 Changing environmental conditions

Conditions such as light and temperature are different in different habitats. These conditions also vary over a 24-hour period.

Marcus wanted to measure changes in temperature in the school greenhouse. He used a <u>datalogger</u> and a thermometer so that he could compare the results. A datalogger collects and records information.

1 Write down <u>two</u> problems of using:

a a thermometer;

b a datalogger.

The charts show Marcus's record of changes in temperature in the greenhouse. He can record daily changes in the amounts of light, sound and water vapour in similar ways.

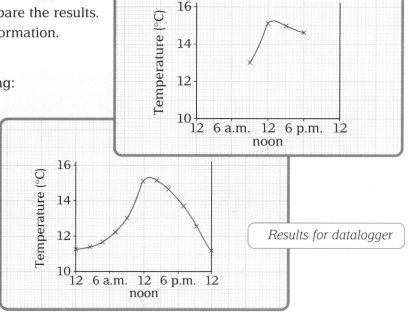

Results for thermometer

Results for datalogger

Like you, other animals are adapted to these daily changes. Some animals are up and about mainly during the day, others at night. Bats and owls are adapted to feed at night. We call them **nocturnal** animals. Some are active when it is getting light or getting dark. So you see different animals at different times.

The chart shows animals seen or heard in a school garden at different times of the day.

Before school	During school	After school	Getting dark	After dark
Squirrels	Butterflies	Butterflies	Sparrows	Bats
Sparrows	Bees	Bees	Midges	Foxes
Blackbirds	Sparrows	Squirrels	Bats	Owls
Rabbits	Kestrels	Sparrows	Foxes	Moths
		Kestrels	Mice	Earthworms

2 a When are foxes usually active?

   b When foxes are looking after cubs, they can be seen at any time. Why do you think this is?

3 Describe the different adaptations of bats and owls for hunting at night.

Light affects plants, too.

Owls hear well and can see in dim light.

Livingstone daisies open only in the sunshine.

This bat feeds on the nectar of banana flowers, which are open at night.

Bats send out sounds and listen for echoes using their sensitive ears. Bats that feed on flying insects have small eyes. Bats that feed on nectar have large eyes.

4 Why do you think the banana flower is light coloured, with scented nectar, and is open at night?

7C.3 Investigating woodlice

Science isn't just about what other people have found out. It is also about finding things out for yourself. You can ask questions. Then you can do investigations to find out the answers.

1 Woodlice are mainly found under things such as big stones and dead leaves. There are many possible reasons for this. Write down as many as you can think of.

You can test one of your ideas using a choice chamber. The woodlouse in the picture has a choice between dark and light.

2 The woodlouse is walking around the choice chamber. Where do you think it will stop? Explain your answer.

When you say what you think will happen, you are making a prediction. Scientists often make predictions. Then they test their predictions to see if they are right.

Even if the woodlouse stopped in the side that you predicted for a long time, you couldn't be sure that your prediction was correct for all woodlice. There are many different kinds of woodlice, and within each kind the woodlice vary.

You need to think about variation when you investigate an animal for yourself. You will also need to think about which environmental conditions you will vary and which you will keep the same.

3 Do you think that the three kinds of woodlouse in the picture will behave in <u>exactly</u> the same way? Explain your answer.

4 Write down some environmental conditions that you think affect woodlice.

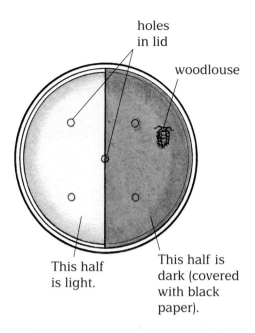

holes in lid

woodlouse

This half is light.

This half is dark (covered with black paper).

A woodlouse in a choice chamber

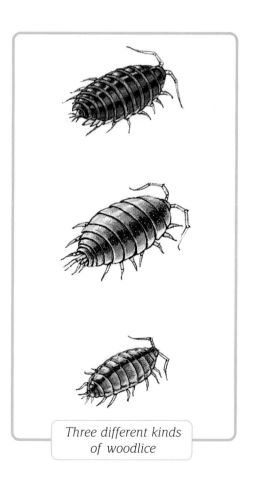

Three different kinds of woodlice

7C.4 Seasonal change

Environmental conditions change with the **seasons**. Plants and animals must be adapted to these changes to survive. In Britain, the cold and frost of winter are problems for many plants and animals. We call these difficult conditions **climatic stresses**. Climatic stresses are different in different parts of the world. In some places the problem is shortage of water; in other places it is high temperatures.

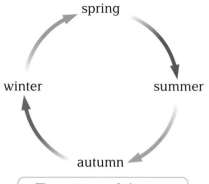

The seasons of the year.

There are fewer hours of daylight in winter.

1 The pictures show the same place in winter and summer. Write down <u>three</u> problems for plants and animals in winter.

Plants lose a lot of water from their leaves. When it is cold, they cannot take any more water in. Also, winter frosts damage some leaves. So, many plants get rid of their leaves before the frosts start.

Other trees keep their leaves all the year round. We say that they are <u>evergreen</u>. Their leaves have to be tough to withstand the cold. They also have a waxy surface so that they don't lose too much water.

2 Write down <u>two</u> advantages of having no leaves in winter.

3 Describe how the leaves of evergreens are adapted to surviving low temperatures and to keeping water in.

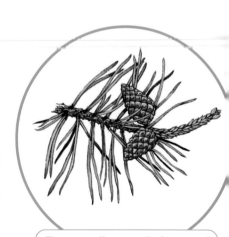

Pine needles aren't damaged by frost and snow.

Plants that lose their leaves can't make food in winter. We say that they are <u>dormant</u>. They use their stores of food to grow new leaves in spring.

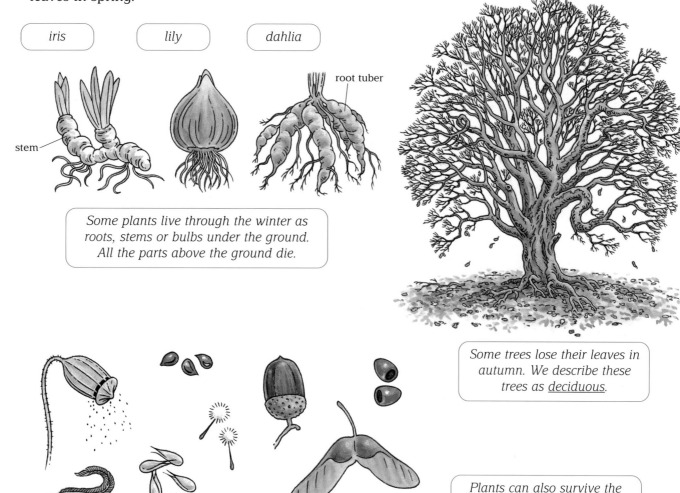

iris   lily   dahlia

stem

root tuber

Some plants live through the winter as roots, stems or bulbs under the ground. All the parts above the ground die.

Some trees lose their leaves in autumn. We describe these trees as <u>deciduous</u>.

Plants can also survive the winter as seeds.

4 Deciduous trees store food in their roots and stems. Why do they need to do this?

5 Only underground parts of some plants survive the winter.

  a Suggest a reason why underground parts of plants are less likely to be killed than leaves.

  b Write down <u>one</u> plant that survives as an underground stem.

6 Find out <u>one</u> adaptation that seeds have to help them survive.

Problems for animals

The British winter brings problems for animals, too. It's cold and there isn't much food, because there are fewer leaves and insects about. Most of the insects that we see in summer live through winter as eggs or pupae. Both of these are hidden away.

Some birds fly south to warmer climates for winter. We say that they **migrate**. Other animals go into a deep sleep called **hibernation**. Their hearts slow down and their temperatures drop. Their bodies slow right down so that stored fat is used up very slowly through winter.

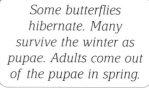

Some butterflies hibernate. Many survive the winter as pupae. Adults come out of the pupae in spring.

When it is winter in Britain, it is warmer in Africa and there are insects for swallows to eat.

During hibernation, hedgehogs use fat stored in their body.

7 Swallows migrate between Africa and Britain. Write down <u>two</u> ways they benefit from this.

Other animals stay active all the year round. In autumn, these birds and mammals store extra fat and grow a thicker coat of fur or feathers for insulation. Some change colour for better **camouflage**.

8 Explain, as fully as you can, how rabbits are adapted to survive winter.

9 Rabbits, swallows and hedgehogs all store up a lot of fat in their body to prepare for winter. Explain how this helps each of them to survive.

Rabbits get fatter and grow a thicker coat to prepare for winter.

7C.5 Feeding relationships

Plants make their own food. Plants are called **producers** because they produce the food. Animals feed on plants or on animals that have eaten plants so we call them **consumers**. Animals that are adapted to eating plants are called **herbivores**. Other animals are adapted to eating animal flesh. They are **carnivores**. Some carnivores hunt and kill living animals. These are **predators**. The animals that they hunt are their **prey**. Prey animals are adapted to escape or to hide from predators.

Predators		Prey	
	owl		snail
	fox		vole
	shark		antelope
	leopard		fly
	spider		rabbit
	eel		plaice
	mantis		greenfly

1 a What is a predator?

2 Sort the predators in the table into groups of animals that:
  ● chase their prey; ● ambush their prey; ● build traps to catch their prey.

3 Write down <u>four</u> adaptations of predators.

4 Write down <u>four</u> adaptations of prey animals.

Food chains

A food chain shows what eats what.

This vole ———▶ is eaten by ———▶ this owl.

Food chains begin with green plants because only green plants make food. The arrows show the direction in which the food goes.

The arrows also show the way that energy is transferred along food chains. When they make food, green plants take energy from sunlight. When an animal eats a plant, the energy is transferred to the animal.

5 Food chains begin with green plants. Explain this as fully as you can.

6 In the food chain, grass ——▶ vole ——▶ owl, name the plant, the predator and the prey.

7 **a** Copy the diagram below. Alongside it draw your own food chain, this time using examples of real plants and animals. Don't forget to include the arrows to show the direction of energy transfer.

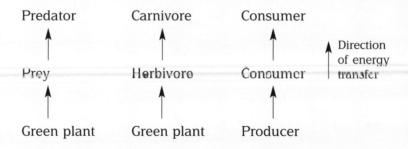

Predator	Carnivore	Consumer
↑	↑	↑
Prey	Herbivore	Consumer
↑	↑	↑
Green plant	Green plant	Producer

Direction of energy transfer

b Notice that the herbivore and the carnivore are both called consumers. The energy is transferred to the herbivore first. So we call it the <u>primary consumer</u>. The carnivore is the second animal to get the energy. So we call it the <u>secondary consumer</u>. Add primary and secondary to your copy of the diagram.

The vole eats plants, so we can add this to the food chain:

This grass

is eaten by

this vole,

which is eaten by

this owl.

7C.6 Food webs

Voles don't feed on grass alone, and owls don't just eat voles. Plants and animals belong to more than one food chain. So, we join food chains to make **food webs** for a habitat.

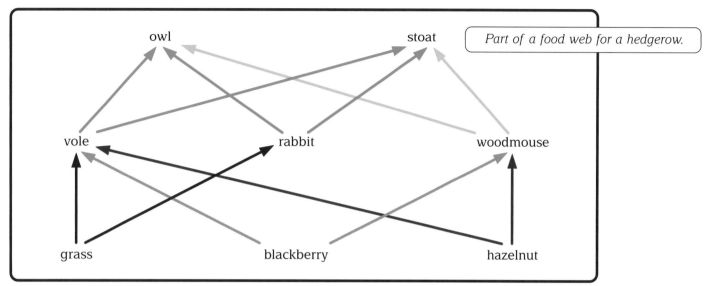

Part of a food web for a hedgerow.

1 **a** Make a copy of the food web. Add your name to it, with arrows to you from the things in it that you can eat.

   b Draw a large arrow next to your copy of the food web to show the direction of energy transfer.

2 Food webs are better than food chains for showing what happens in a habitat. Explain why.

Green plants are at the start of a food web. They transfer energy from sunlight into the web as food. So, if all the plants disappear, there is no food for the animals in the habitat.

A change in the number of animals also affects food webs. For example, the following things will happen if all the owls die.

- The population of animals that the owls usually eat will go up.

- Then there will be more food for stoats, and the population of stoats will go up.

- Rabbits, voles and mice **compete** for food. If there are too many of them, some won't get enough to eat. They will die.

3 **a** From the food web above, write down <u>two</u> animals that compete to eat rabbits.

   b Suppose all the rabbits catch a disease and die. Write down <u>two</u> effects that this would have on the food web. Explain your answer.

You should now have an understanding of these key ideas. You should also be able to spell and to know the meaning of the key words. The **key words** are in **bold** on this page.

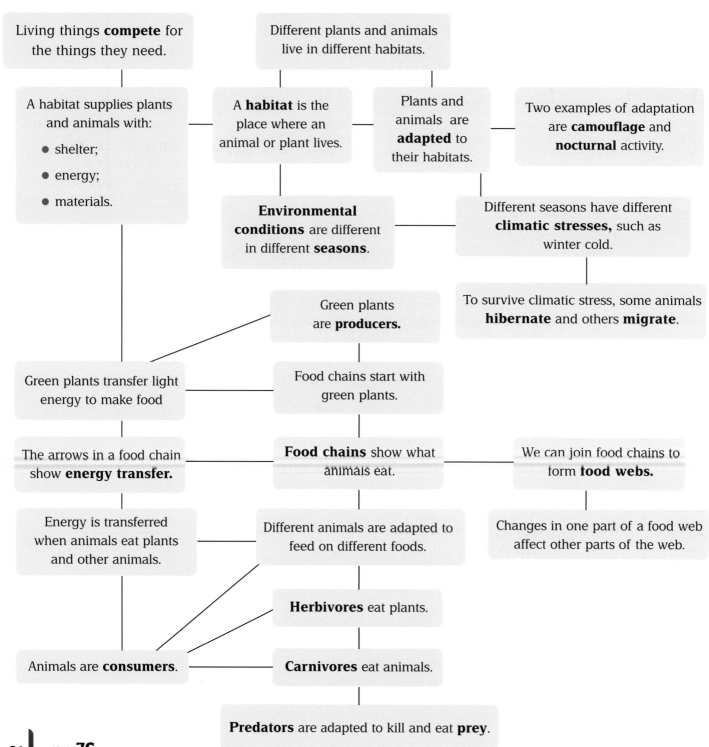

Living things **compete** for the things they need.

Different plants and animals live in different habitats.

A habitat supplies plants and animals with:
- shelter;
- energy;
- materials.

A **habitat** is the place where an animal or plant lives.

Plants and animals are **adapted** to their habitats.

Two examples of adaptation are **camouflage** and **nocturnal** activity.

Environmental conditions are different in different **seasons**.

Different seasons have different **climatic stresses,** such as winter cold.

To survive climatic stress, some animals **hibernate** and others **migrate**.

Green plants are **producers.**

Green plants transfer light energy to make food

Food chains start with green plants.

The arrows in a food chain show **energy transfer.**

Food chains show what animals eat.

We can join food chains to form **food webs.**

Energy is transferred when animals eat plants and other animals.

Different animals are adapted to feed on different foods.

Changes in one part of a food web affect other parts of the web.

Herbivores eat plants.

Animals are **consumers**.

Carnivores eat animals.

Predators are adapted to kill and eat **prey**.

Variation and classification

In this unit we shall be studying some similarities and differences between species. We shall look at variation within species and consider the causes of it. We shall also look at how and why scientists sort living things into groups.

KEY WORDS

species
characteristics
vary
variations
inherited variations
environmental
  variations
family tree
classification
vertebrates
invertebrates
fish
amphibians
reptiles
birds
mammals
arthropods

7D.1 The same but different

A **species** is one kind of living thing.

Members of a species:

- are very much alike (we say that a lot of their **characteristics** are the same);

- are different from members of other species;

- produce fertile offspring only when they breed with each other.

Humans are all similar. They can mate with each other and produce fertile offspring. So we say that they belong to the same species.

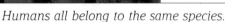
Humans all belong to the same species.

1 Why do we group all humans together as one species?

2 Write down <u>four</u> characteristics of all humans.

Variety is the spice of life!

Even though humans share many characteristics, there are differences between them. We say that they **vary**. We call the differences **variations**. Some of the differences are easy to see. Other differences are difficult or impossible to see.

3 Write down <u>three</u> differences between the people in the photograph.

4 Look at these pictures of girls. Write down <u>two</u> differences that you can see. Write down <u>one</u> difference that you cannot see.

> All these girls have different blood groups.

Variations in other animals and plants

We have seen how humans vary. We can see variations in other animals, too. The dogs in the pictures below look different because they are different breeds. But they are all members of the same species.

basset hound   terrier   labrador

offspring 1   offspring 2   offspring 3

pup 1   pup 2

> A family tree for a basset hound, a terrier, a labrador and their offspring.

5 Write down:

   a <u>four</u> characteristics of dogs;

   b how each of these characteristics varies.

6 How do you know that the breeds of dogs in the pictures belong to the same species?

Plants from the same species also vary. Corn is one species of plant. Its fruits are called cobs. Corncobs come in several different shapes, sizes and colours. We call these <u>varieties of corn</u>.

> *Corn is a species belonging to the grass family.*

Look at the pictures of corncobs. We use different varieties for sweetcorn, animal food, popcorn, cornflour and cornflakes.

> *Different varieties of corncobs*

7 Write down <u>three</u> variations between the cobs in the pictures.

8 Explain how we can prove that all the cobs belong to the same species.

7D.2 The causes of variation

Variations in a characteristic often run in families. They are passed from one generation to the next. We call them **inherited variations**. But not all variations are inherited. Some characteristics vary because of the environment in which a living thing develops. These variations are called **environmental variations**. Other variations have a mixture of inherited and environmental causes.

Emperor Maximillian (1459–1519)

Maximillian's grandson, Emperor Charles V (1500–1558)

Variations that run in families

The Habsburg family was one of the ruling families of Europe. Many members had a lip that was characteristic of the family. It is called the Habsburg lip.

1 Look carefully at the pictures of the Habsburg family members. Describe the Habsburg lip.

Archduke Charles of Teschen (1771–1847)

2 What other information would be useful to decide if this characteristic was inherited in the Habsburg family?

How we find patterns of inheritance

We can use a diagram to show how people are related to each other. We call this diagram a **family tree**. A family tree can also show how a characteristic is inherited. We can see if a characteristic passes from parents to children. A characteristic is inherited when we see a strong pattern in a family tree.

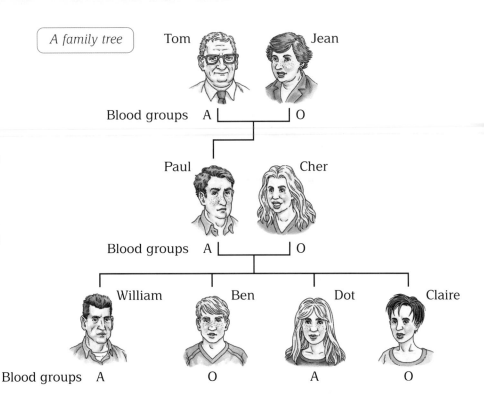

A family tree

Tom   Jean

Blood groups   A |_____| O

Paul   Cher

Blood groups   A |_____| O

William   Ben   Dot   Claire

Blood groups   A   O   A   O

3 Look at the family tree. How many generations does it show?

4 Write down <u>two</u> ways in which Paul is similar to his parents.

5 Write down <u>two</u> other characteristics that are inherited in this family.

6 For each statement, say whether it is TRUE or FALSE. In each case, write down <u>one</u> piece of evidence.

   a Boys always inherit characteristics only from their fathers.

   b Some characteristics seem to miss one generation.

   c Children are identical to their parents.

   d Children of the same family can be very different.

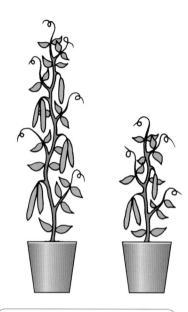

Environmental variations

Environmental variations are not inherited. They develop as a result of what happens to an animal or plant during its lifetime.

7 The pea plants in the pictures inherited different characteristics. Explain how we know this.

These pea plants grew in exactly the same environmental conditions.

This is how leeks grow. These leeks are all the same variety.

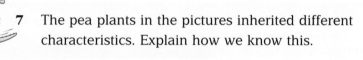

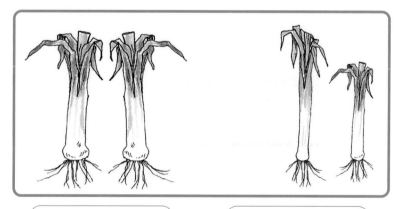

Leeks from the centre of the garden

Leeks from the edge of the garden

8 Write down <u>three</u> differences in the environment that could have caused the variation in the leeks in the picture.

Joan and Ellen are identical twins. Ellen had a serious illness when she was nine. So she did not grow as tall as her sister.

9 Look at the picture of the identical twins. Write down <u>two</u> characteristics of Joan and Ellen caused only by:

a inheritance;

b the environment.

10 Height is partly an inherited and partly an environmental variation. Use the information you know about Joan and Ellen to explain this.

7D.3 Describing living things

We have seen that there can be lots of variation between members of the same species. But there is more variation between members of different species. Gorillas have similarities to humans, but they also have key characteristics that are different from those of humans. So gorillas belong to a different species.

1 Look carefully at the pictures. Write down <u>three</u> differences between the human and the gorilla.

When you look for differences between a human and a gorilla, you have to look carefully. Careful observation is very important in science.

Books for identifying plants and animals use drawings and detailed descriptions to help us to tell one species from another. Descriptions in stories and poems don't have to be so accurate. They are sometimes about only one characteristic.

Gorilla

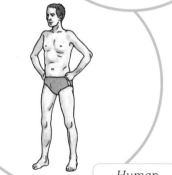

Human

2 Read the poem. Write down <u>three</u> animals that could fit the description in the poem.

There once was a ——————— called Nick
whose movements were sudden and quick.
He loved to pop out
and cause people to shout
but his wriggling legs made me sick!

3 Now read the description of the same animal below. What type of animal do you think it is now?

Nick has eight legs.
He has two parts to his body, a head and an <u>abdomen</u>.
He has <u>spinnerets</u> that he uses to make silken threads.
He has hard outer parts called an <u>exoskeleton</u> to protect him.
Nick eats insects, so he is a <u>carnivore</u>.

4 **a** Write down <u>one</u> piece of information about Nick's structure that is in the poem.

 b The description gives you more information about this part. Write down that extra information.

5 What does the poem tell you about Nick that is not in the description?

6 Make a list of the special words used in the description. Then match them with the definitions below.

 a An animal that eats other animals.

 b The tail end of the body, often swollen.

 c A skeleton on the outside of a body.

 d Tiny finger-like body parts that make silken threads.

Why details are important

Hoverflies and wasps look similar in many ways. However, wasps sting, but hoverflies don't. Many people like to see hoverflies in their gardens because hoverfly young eat the greenfly that damage their plants.

7 Why is it useful to be able to tell the difference between a wasp and a hoverfly?

Hoverfly

Scientific description of hoverflies	Scientific description of common wasps
Hoverflies have a head, a thorax and an abdomen.	Common wasps have a head, a thorax and an abdomen.
Hoverflies have six jointed legs.	Common wasps have six jointed legs.
Hoverflies have bright black-and-yellow markings on their abdomens.	Common wasps have bright black-and-yellow markings on their abdomens.
Hoverflies often feed on pollen and nectar from flowers.	Common wasps like sugary foods but mainly feed on meat.
Hoverflies can hover.	Common wasps do not hover.
Hoverflies have a margin on the edge of their wings.	Common wasps do not have a margin on the edge of their wings.
Hoverflies have large, round compound eyes.	Common wasps have crescent-shaped eyes.
Hoverflies do not have jaws.	Common wasps have jaws for biting.
Hoverflies do not have a sting.	Common wasps have a sting.

Common wasp

8 Look at the table. Write down <u>three</u> characteristics that hoverflies and common wasps share.

9 Write down <u>two</u> characteristics that would help you to tell the difference between a hoverfly and a common wasp.

10 Explain why looking at details is important when we describe animals such as these insects.

11 Look at the picture of a centipede and a millipede and use the words below to write a description of each one.

- **Jointed leg:** leg with more than one joint (or bend) along its length.
- **Segments:** sections along the body.
- **Antenna:** long, thin projection on the head.

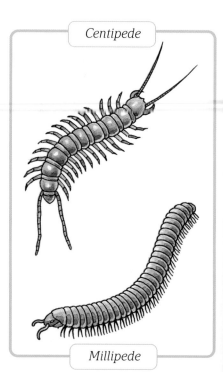

Centipede

Millipede

7D.4 Sorting things into groups

We often sort things into groups to make them easier to deal with. For example, the police have files containing millions of fingerprints. They use them to identify fingerprints found at crime scenes. If the fingerprints can be sorted into groups with similar characteristics, only one group of fingerprints needs to be checked, rather than all of them.

whorl

Whorls | Loops | Arches

1 Which file do you think the police will check to identify the fingerprint in the picture?

There are lots of ways of sorting living things. Some ways are more useful than others. We often start by sorting them into green plants and animals.

living things
green plants   animals

2 You know from what you learned in Unit 7A that plant and animal cells are different. What else do you know about green plants and animals that helps you to fit them into their groups?

Then we sort these groups into smaller groups. These pictures show one way of sorting animals into groups.

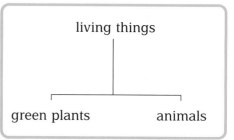
sparrow   eagle
bat
fly   owl

These land animals can fly.

crab
fish
octopus
shark
whale

These animals live in water.

spider   hamster   humans
badger
cat   horse

3 Explain why these groups are not a very useful way of sorting these animals.

4 Write down <u>two</u> animals that are separated in these groups but that you think should be in a group together.

5 Sort the animals in the picture into <u>two</u> groups using a different characteristic.

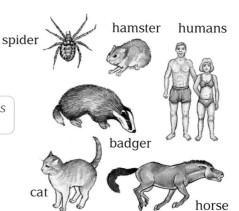

These animals live on land.

7D.5 Sorting plants and animals

Scientists have named and described several million different species of plants and animals. They think that millions more will be discovered in the future. We can't learn about every one of them. So we sort them into groups with lots of characteristics in common. We call this sorting **classification**.

For example, birds have feathers, beaks and wings and they walk on two legs. So if we are told that an eagle is a bird, we already know a lot of things about it. You might see an animal that you haven't seen before, but you might know that it is a bird. So you look it up in a book about birds, rather than a book about all animals.

1   Write down <u>three</u> facts about an eagle.

2   What do we call it when we sort things into groups?

3   Why do we sort living things into groups?

Aristotle lived in Greece over 2000 years ago. He was the first person to use sets of characteristics of animals and plants to sort them into groups. Before Aristotle, people grouped animals into land and water animals or winged and wingless animals.

Aristotle saw that some ants have wings and others don't. So he realised that a simple grouping into winged and wingless animals doesn't work.

Aristotle (384–322 BC)

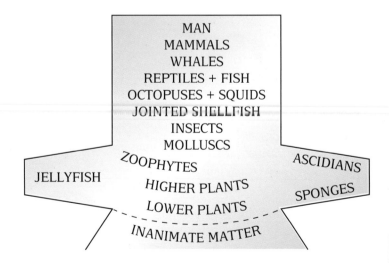

MAN
MAMMALS
WHALES
REPTILES + FISH
OCTOPUSES + SQUIDS
JOINTED SHELLFISH
INSECTS
MOLLUSCS
ZOOPHYTES
JELLYFISH
HIGHER PLANTS
ASCIDIANS
SPONGES
LOWER PLANTS
INANIMATE MATTER

Aristotle's classification system.

4   Why do you think Aristotle used sets of characteristics for his classification system?

Now we sort living things into groups that have lots of characteristics in common. Scientists all over the world use the same system. When they find a new animal or plant, they look at similarities and differences between it and known animals. Then they fit it into a group. Sometimes they have to change the groupings a bit.

5 Look at the pictures of the eagle, the bat and the dragonfly below. Write down <u>one</u> similarity and <u>one</u> difference between the eagle and the bat.

Bat

Dragonfly

Eagle

Birds have feathers, but other animal groups don't. So feathers are a useful characteristic for identifying an animal as a bird. Birds, bats and many insects fly. But bats and insects are very different from birds. So flying is not a useful characteristic for classifying animals.

6 Some characteristics are more useful than others for classifying. Look at the pictures of the eagle, the bat and the dragonfly. Having feathers is a better characteristic than flying to tell birds apart from other animals. Why is this?

7 Why is it useful for all scientists to use the same classification system?

Classifying animals

Some animals have skeletons made of bone inside their bodies. Scientists classify all these animals in a group called **vertebrates**. We sometimes call them <u>animals with backbones</u>.

8 The skeletons of different vertebrates have lots of characteristics in common. Write down <u>three</u> similarities between the skeletons of the human and the mole in these pictures.

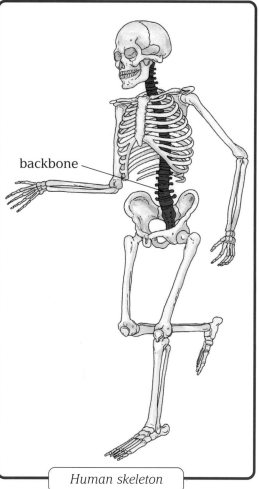

backbone

Human skeleton

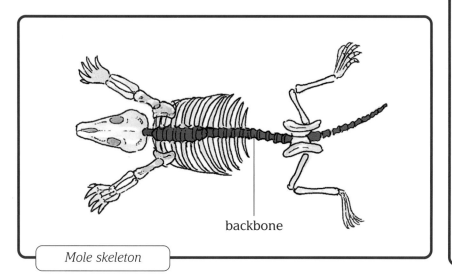

backbone

Mole skeleton

Animals without backbones are called **invertebrates**. Some of them have hard body parts, but these are different from vertebrate skeletons.

A snail is an invertebrate with a shell.

A crab is an invertebrate. Its jointed skeleton is on the outside of its body.

9 Describe the hard body parts of <u>two</u> invertebrates.

Vertebrates

There are about 60 000 different species of vertebrates that we know about, so we divide them into smaller groups.

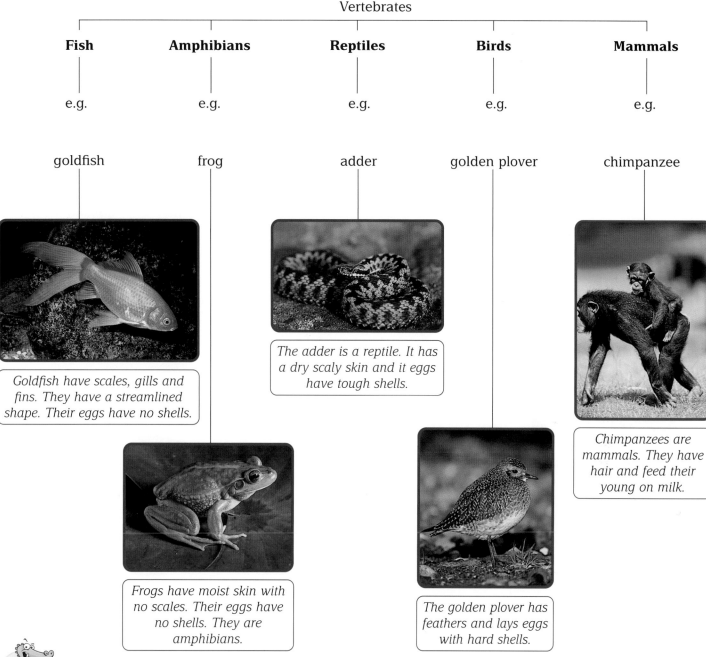

Vertebrates

| Fish | Amphibians | Reptiles | Birds | Mammals |

e.g.   e.g.   e.g.   e.g.   e.g.

goldfish   frog   adder   golden plover   chimpanzee

Goldfish have scales, gills and fins. They have a streamlined shape. Their eggs have no shells.

The adder is a reptile. It has a dry scaly skin and it eggs have tough shells.

Chimpanzees are mammals. They have hair and feed their young on milk.

Frogs have moist skin with no scales. Their eggs have no shells. They are amphibians.

The golden plover has feathers and lays eggs with hard shells.

10 Look carefully at the diagram and pictures above.
Write down <u>one</u> characteristic that all these animals share.

11 What makes mammals different from the other groups of vertebrates?

12 Write down <u>two</u> differences between amphibians and reptiles.

13 Newts are amphibians. From this information only, write down <u>two</u> things that you know about newts.

Invertebrates

Over nine tenths of all species of animals don't have bones. They are classified as invertebrates. We divide them into groups, too.

Invertebrates

Jellyfish e.g. sea anemone	Molluscs e.g. snail	Flatworms e.g. planarian and tapeworm	True worms e.g. earthworm	**Arthropods** e.g. spider
jelly-like body, stinging cells	shell, one muscular foot	flat body, not divided into segments	round body, divided into segments	hard parts on outside, jointed legs, segmented body

14 Write down <u>one</u> characteristic that all invertebrates share.

15 Look carefully at the diagram. The planarian and the earthworm are in different groups. Write down <u>two</u> differences between them.

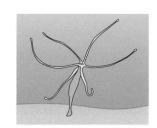

Hydra

Snail

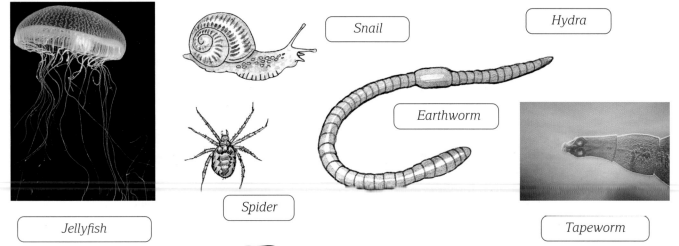

Earthworm

Jellyfish

Spider

Tapeworm

Planarian

16 The hydra and the jellyfish belong to the same group of invertebrates. Write down <u>two</u> characteristics that they share.

17 The ragworm is in the same invertebrate group as the earthworm. Explain why these animals are classified in the same group.

Ragworm

More groups

All the groups that we have studied so far are very big. So we divide them into smaller groups. More than three quarters of all animal species are arthropods. We divide these animals into four main groups.

Crab

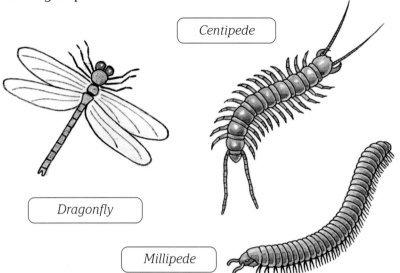

Centipede

Dragonfly

Millipede

Lobster

Fly

18 Look carefully at the pictures of arthropods.
Write down <u>two</u> characteristics that all arthropods share.

Erigone

19 What <u>two</u> characteristics could you use to split this big group?

Arthropod group	What do they look like?
Crustaceans	Two pairs of antennae; five or more pairs of legs
Insects	Three pairs of legs; one or two pairs of wings
Spiders	Four pairs of legs; no antennae
Myriapods (many legs)	Long body divided into segments; legs on every segment

20 Look carefully at the pictures and the table.

   a Which invertebrate group do these animals belong to?

   dragonfly   centipede   crab   *Erigone*

   b Explain why you chose the group you did for each animal.

You should now understand the key words and key ideas shown below.

Key words

species	invertebrates
characteristics	fish
vary	amphibians
variations	reptiles
inherited variations	birds
environmental variations	mammals
family tree	arthropods
classification	
vertebrates	

Key ideas

- A species is one kind of living thing.
- Members of a species breed with each other to produce fertile offspring.
- Members of a species have a lot of characteristics in common.
- Individuals of the same species vary.
- Variations that pass from parents to offspring are called inherited variations.
- Differences caused by the conditions in which the plant or animal lives are called environmental variations. They are not passed on to offspring.

- Sorting things into groups is called classification. We put living things with the same characteristics in a group.
- We divide large groups into smaller groups.
- Scientists all over the world use the same classification system. This means that they all know which animals or plants they are writing about.

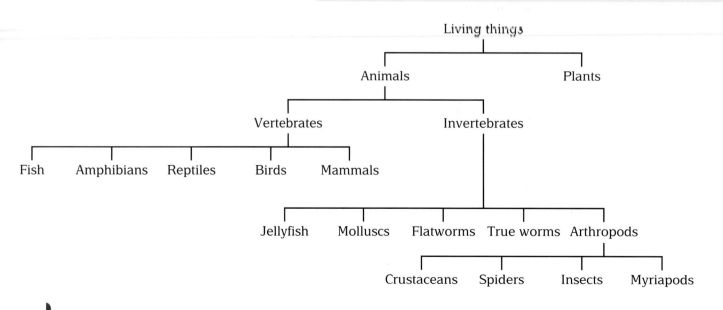

Acids and alkalis

In this unit we shall be finding out about acids and alkalis and how to recognise them. We shall also look at some uses of acids and alkalis and at neutralisation reactions.

7E.1 What acids and alkalis are like

Acids are all around us

It is amazing how many things around us contain **acids**. Some acids are in the food we eat. We use acids to make things work properly and to make all sorts of useful items. Some acids are harmless, but others are very dangerous.

*Fruit or drinks made from fruit often contain acids. They have a tangy, sharp taste. We say acids taste **sour**.*

KEY WORDS

acid
sour
hydrochloric acid
hazard
corrosive
dilute
harmful
irritant
risk
alkali
sodium hydroxide
extract
indicator
**full-range universal
  indicator**
pH scale
neutral
react
neutralisation
salt
indigestion

1 Look at the picture.
   Write down a list of
   substances that contain acids.

2 Write down:

   a <u>one</u> word that best describes the acid taste of lemon juice;

   b the name of the acid that gives lemon juice this taste.

3 **a** What is the name of the other acid in limes and lemons?

   b What disorder does this acid help to prevent?

Limes and lemons taste sour because they contain citric acid. Lemons and limes prevent scurvy because they contain vitamin C. Vitamin C is also an acid, but it is a very weak acid.

Some acids are dangerous

Not all acids are the same. Fruit juice is not dangerous but there are some acids that can be risky to use. Substances like **hydrochloric acid** have their own **hazard** warning sign. Hazard warning signs let people know that they need to be careful. People who use hazardous chemicals must protect themselves and others.

The particular hazard of hydrochloric acid is that it is **corrosive**. This means that it will immediately attack your skin and start eating it away. The hazard warning sign shows this.

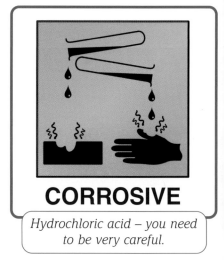

CORROSIVE

Hydrochloric acid – you need to be very careful.

4 Look at the hazard warning sign for hydrochloric acid. What does the word 'corrosive' mean?

If you get hydrochloric acid on yourself, you should wash the area with lots of water. When you mix acid with water, we say that you **dilute** it. This makes the acid less dangerous.

You also need to be careful with dilute hydrochloric acid. Dilute acids are **harmful** or **irritant**, so we use a black cross to warn people about their risks.

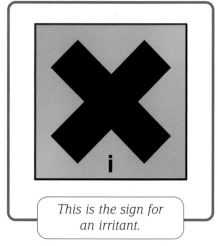

This is the sign for an irritant.

5 If you spill hydrochloric acid on your skin:

   a what can happen?

   b what do you need to do?

   Explain your answers.

6 Why must you always wear eye protection when you use hydrochloric acid?

This is the sign for a harmful substance.

About alkalis

The group of chemicals shown in the picture are not acids but they do react with acids. These substances are **alkalis**. When acids and alkalis react, their properties are cancelled out.

We make soap using alkali and oils. Your skin contains oils. When you get alkali on your skin, your skin oils react with the alkali and your skin feels soapy as it dissolves away. We call the wound a chemical burn.

> *All these substances contain alkalis.*

7 Make a list of household substances which contain alkalis.

Some alkalis are safe to use. Others, such as **sodium hydroxide,** are just as dangerous as the strongest acids.

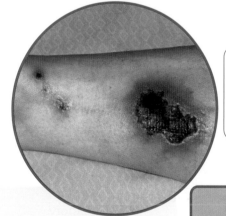

> *Alkalis can be dangerous. These burns were caused by caustic soda. Caustic soda is also known as sodium hydroxide.*

8 What is the hazard symbol on the bottle of bleach?

9 What do you need to do if bleach accidentally gets into your eyes?

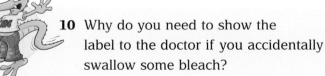

10 Why do you need to show the label to the doctor if you accidentally swallow some bleach?

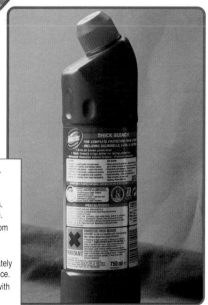

THICK BLEACH CONTAINS SODIUM HYDROXIDE.

Irritating to eyes and skin.

Warning Do not use with other products. May release dangerous gases (chlorine).

Store upright in a cool safe place away from babies, children and animals.

Avoid contact with skin and eyes.

In case of contact with eyes, rinse immediately with plenty of water and seek medical advice.

After contact with skin wash immediately with plenty of clean water.

IF SWALLOWED SEEK MEDICAL ADVICE IMMEDIATELY AND SHOW THIS CONTAINER LABEL.

Uses of acids and alkalis

We find acids and alkalis in many natural substances.
The chemical industry makes millions of tonnes of acids
and alkalis every year.

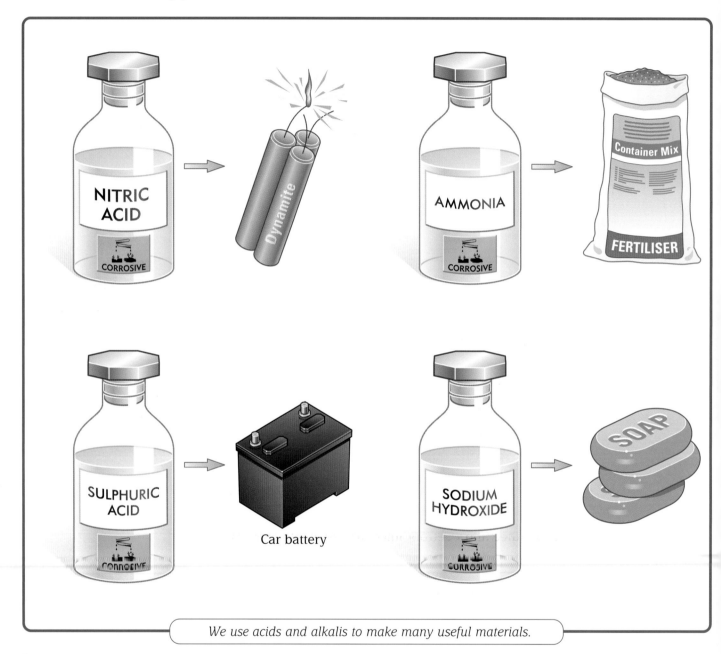

We use acids and alkalis to make many useful materials.

11 Name the acid or alkali used to make:

    a car batteries;

    b explosives;

    c soap;

    d fertilisers.

7E.2 Telling acids and alkalis apart

Sodium hydroxide, hydrochloric acid, lemonade and water are all colourless liquids. They <u>look</u> the same, but they are really very different substances.

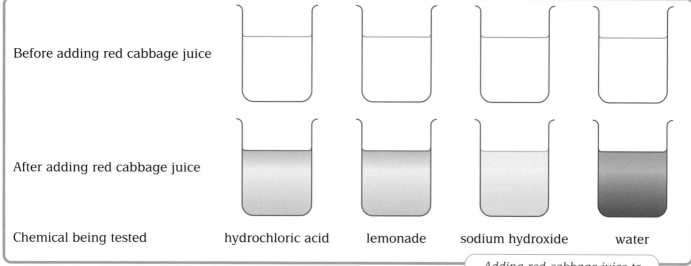

Before adding red cabbage juice				
After adding red cabbage juice				
Chemical being tested	hydrochloric acid	lemonade	sodium hydroxide	water

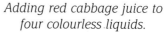
Adding red cabbage juice to four colourless liquids.

1 Look at the pictures. What colour does red cabbage juice turn when added to:

    a hydrochloric acid;   **b** lemonade;

    c sodium hydroxide;   **d** water?

2 Is lemonade an acid or an alkali? Explain your answer.

We can use the colour change of red cabbage juice to show if a substance is an acid or alkali. We can use juices from some other plants too. We call plant juices **extracts**.

- Red cabbage juice and beetroot juice are vegetable extracts.
- Blackcurrant juice is a fruit extract.
- Litmus is extracted from a lichen.

All these extracts change colour to show or <u>indicate</u> whether a substance is an acid, an alkali or neutral. So we call them **indicators**.

3 Name <u>two</u> indicators that can be made from vegetables.

4 What is an extract?

5 Find out what lichen is.

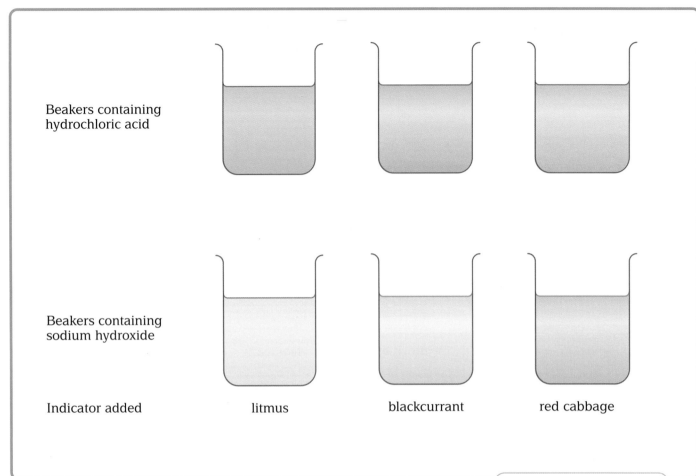

Beakers containing hydrochloric acid

Beakers containing sodium hydroxide

Indicator added

litmus   blackcurrant   red cabbage

The effect of hydrochloric acid and sodium hydroxide on some indicators.

6 Is sodium hydroxide an acid or an alkali?

7 What colour do the following indicators turn when added to hydrochloric acid?

  a blackcurrant;

  b litmus;

  c red cabbage.

8 What colour do the following indicators turn when added to sodium hydroxide?

  a blackcurrant;

  b litmus;

  c red cabbage.

9 What do some plant extracts do that makes them useful indicators?

7E.3 Universal indicator and the pH scale

All the indicators that we have looked at so far only tell us if a substance is an acid or an alkali. Lemonade and hydrochloric acid have the same effect on all these indicators, but they have a very different effect if you spill them on your skin.

1 Luke tells his teacher that he can tell the difference between lemonade and hydrochloric acid very easily. 'All you have to do is taste them.' If you were Luke's teacher what would you tell him?

Full-range universal indicator is a special type of indicator that is made by combining lots of different indicators together. We can use it to show if something is acid, alkaline or neutral. But we can also use it to show if something is strongly acidic like hydrochloric acid or weakly acidic like lemonade. In the same way, we can use it to tell whether an alkali is weak or strong.

2 Water is a neutral substance. What colour do you get when you add a few drops of universal indicator to a test-tube of water?

Scientists actually measure the strengths of acids and alkalis on a scale from 0 to 14 known as the **pH scale**. They match the indicator colours to the numbers on the pH scale.

On the pH scale numbers between 0 and 6 are for acids and numbers from 8 to 14 are for alkalis. The number 7 is neither acid nor alkali – we say that it is **neutral**.

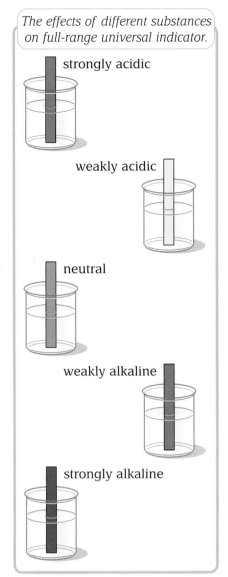

The effects of different substances on full-range universal indicator.

strongly acidic

weakly acidic

neutral

weakly alkaline

strongly alkaline

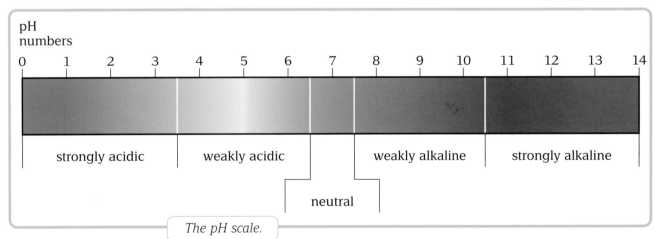

pH numbers

0 1 2 3 4 5 6 7 8 9 10 11 12 13 14

strongly acidic   weakly acidic   weakly alkaline   strongly alkaline

neutral

The pH scale.

3   What do you think the pH of each of the following substances will be?

   a Strongly acidic hydrochloric acid;

   b Weakly acidic lemonade;

   c Strongly alkaline sodium hydroxide.

4   What colour will full-range universal indicator go if you add it to the following substances?

   a potassium hydroxide, pH = 12;

   b soda water, pH = 5;

   c sulphuric acid, pH = 2.

5   A beaker of concentrated hydrochloric acid has a pH of 1.

   a What colour will full-range universal indicator turn if it is added to the beaker?

   b Is concentrated hydrochloric acid strongly or weakly acidic?

6   A group of pupils tested a range of chemicals but they lost some of their results and so they could not complete the table. To help them, answer the questions.

Substance	Colour with full-range universal indicator	pH	Type of substance
nitric acid	red	1	strongly acidic
vinegar		5	
ammonia	purple		
sodium bicarbonate	blue		weakly alkaline
salt water	green	7	

   a What colour was the full-range universal indicator in vinegar?

   b What is a possible value for the pH value of ammonia?

   c What type of substance is salt water?

   d What is the possible value for the pH of sodium bicarbonate?

7E.4 Neutralisation and the rainbow experiment

When an acid and an alkali are mixed together a chemical reaction happens. The acid **reacts** with the alkali to cancel it out. This reaction is called **neutralisation**.

About neutralisation

During a neutralisation reaction the pH of a solution changes. This is because the acid and the alkali cancel each other out. This produces a neutral substance called a **salt**. Water is also produced. Neutralisation is an important chemical reaction.

acid + alkali → salt + water

If exactly the right amount of acid is added to an alkali the solution produced is neutral. However, if too much acid is added the solution will become acidic.

1   What happens when too little acid is added to an alkali?

The rainbow experiment is an example of a neutralisation reaction actually taking place. In this experiment, you put a washing soda crystal into a test-tube full of water. Washing soda is an alkali. Its scientific name is sodium carbonate.

You add hydrochloric acid to almost fill the test-tube, then a few drops of full-range universal indicator.

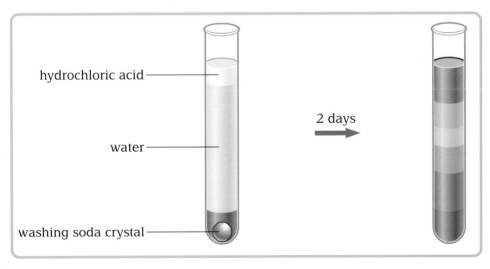

hydrochloric acid

water

2 days

washing soda crystal

2   a What colour is the solution close to the washing soda crystal?

    b Are washing soda crystals acid or alkaline?

3 a After 2 or 3 days what is the pH of the solution at the top of the test-tube?

   b Part of the solution has turned yellow. What will the pH of the solution be here?

   c Both the yellow section and the top of the test-tube are acidic. What is the difference between them?

4 In the blue part of the solution, is there more acid present or more alkali?

In the rainbow experiment the hydrochloric acid has slowly moved down the test-tube. The washing soda crystal has dissolved and the alkaline solution has moved up the test-tube. Neutralisation takes place where the two solutions meet.

5 After 2 or 3 days there is a small part of the solution which is green. Is this part of the solution acidic, alkaline or neutral?

6 Andrew tried to do the rainbow experiment, but after 2 or 3 days his test-tube was completely purple. What can he do to get a rainbow?

The rainbow experiment.

What happens with other acids and alkalis?

There are many examples of neutralisation reactions with acids and alkalis. In each of these a salt is produced, as well as water. The salt produced depends on which acids and alkalis are used.

We can describe what has happened by using a <u>word equation</u>.

| hydrochloric acid | + | sodium hydroxide | → | sodium chloride | + | water |

The name of the salt depends on the acid and the alkali:

- hydrochloric acid gives <u>chloride</u>
- sodium hydroxide gives <u>sodium</u>

to give the salt <u>sodium chloride</u>.

7 If we used potassium hydroxide instead of sodium hydroxide what salt would we make?

7E.5 Where neutralisation is important

Neutralisation is a very important reaction in our daily lives.

Curing indigestion

Indigestion is often caused by too much acid in the stomach. You can take medicine to neutralise this acid. Some contain a weak alkali called magnesium hydroxide. Other indigestion cures contain magnesium carbonate or sodium bicarbonate. These neutralise acids but also make carbon dioxide, which is a gas.

1 What causes indigestion?

2 Sodium hydroxide solution has a pH of 14.
Why can't you use sodium hydroxide to cure indigestion?

Sarah and her class decided to investigate some indigestion remedies to see if they were any good. Look at their table of results.

Tablet	Cost per tablet	Amount of acid neutralised	Amount of gas produced	Time taken to neutralise the acid
Brand A	3p	25 cm^3	none	3 minutes
Brand B	4p	20 cm^3	none	10 minutes
Brand C	5p	30 cm^3	15 cm^3	2 minutes
Brand D	1p	10 cm^3	28 cm^3	1 minute
Brand E	8p	40 cm^3	15 cm^3	2 minutes

3 **a** Which tablet neutralises the most acid?

b Which is the cheapest tablet?

c Which tablet works more slowly than all the others?

4 **a** What is the name of the gas produced?

b What is the name of <u>one</u> substance which makes this gas?

5 What happens if you take an indigestion tablet that makes a lot of gas?

6 Which indigestion tablet do you think you should use? Explain your answer.

7 Sarah found it hard to measure the amount of acid that Brand E neutralised because the tablets were red. Why is it hard to do the experiment with red tablets?

Other uses of neutralisation reactions

Toothpaste

Your mouth is full of bacteria. These feed on any food left in your mouth. These bacteria then produce acid in your mouth. The acid can attack your teeth, making them decay. When you brush your teeth the alkali in toothpaste neutralises the acid. This helps to protect your teeth.

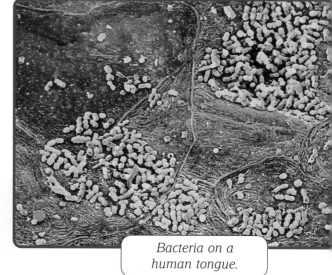

Bacteria on a human tongue.

8 Your saliva is slightly alkaline. What effect will saliva have on the amount of acid in your mouth?

9 Dentists recommend chewing sugar-free gum after meals. Why do you think this helps reduce tooth decay. (Hint: Chewing causes lots of saliva to be produced.)

Making cakes rise

Baking powder is an ingredient in some cake recipes. It contains both an acid and an alkali. The alkali is called bicarbonate of soda. When the acid neutralises the bicarbonate of soda the gas carbon dioxide is produced. It is this gas that produces the bubbles in sponge cakes.

The pH of this toothpaste is 8 because it contains bicarbonate of soda.

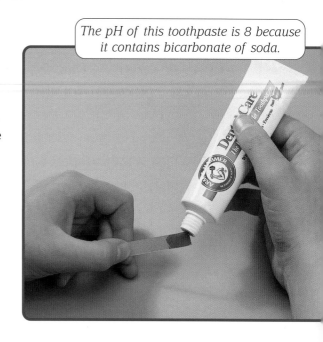

Acid rain

Some factories and power stations pollute the air with gases that cause acid rain. Rainwater dissolves these acid gases so that its pH is lower than 7. Acid rain can harm the environment.

Soil treatment

The pH of soil is different in different places. In some areas the soil is too acidic for plants to grow well and therefore lime is added. Lime raises the pH because it is an alkali. Lime is also called calcium oxide. It will neutralise some of the acid in the soil. This means that the pH of the soil is raised, making it less acidic. Plants can now grow well.

Often, calcium carbonate is added to lakes because it neutralises the acid that comes from the rain water.

10 Write down <u>three</u> examples of uses of neutralisation.

11 Potatoes grow well on Jim's farm, which has soil with a pH of 5.5. He decides to add lime to his soil so he can grow broccoli instead.

   a Do potatoes grow better in acid or alkaline soil?

   b Does broccoli grow better in acid or alkaline soil?

12 a What are the advantages and disadvantages of adding lime to the soil?

   b Why do you think Jim decided to grow broccoli?

You should now understand the key words and key ideas shown below.

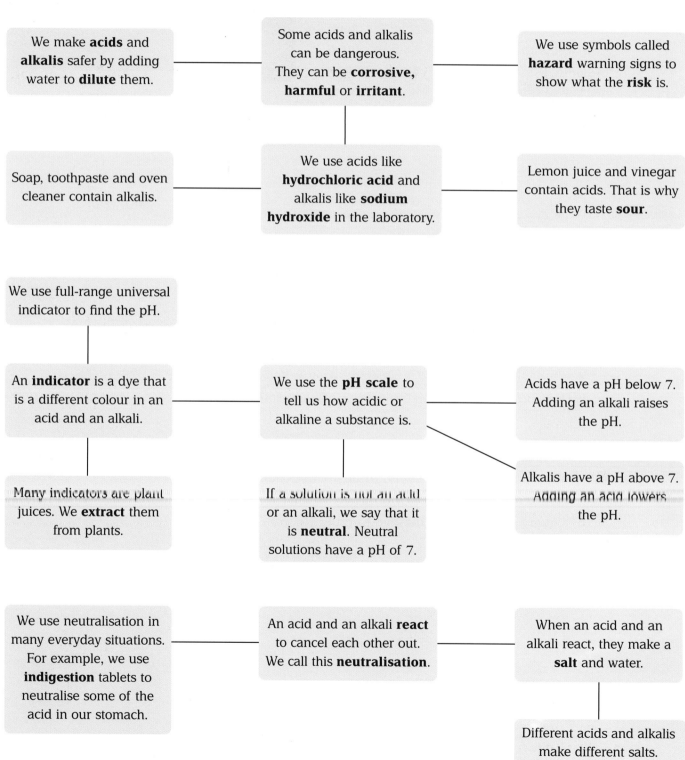

We make **acids** and **alkalis** safer by adding water to **dilute** them.

Some acids and alkalis can be dangerous. They can be **corrosive, harmful** or **irritant**.

We use symbols called **hazard** warning signs to show what the **risk** is.

Soap, toothpaste and oven cleaner contain alkalis.

We use acids like **hydrochloric acid** and alkalis like **sodium hydroxide** in the laboratory.

Lemon juice and vinegar contain acids. That is why they taste **sour**.

We use full-range universal indicator to find the pH.

An **indicator** is a dye that is a different colour in an acid and an alkali.

We use the **pH scale** to tell us how acidic or alkaline a substance is.

Acids have a pH below 7. Adding an alkali raises the pH.

Many indicators are plant juices. We **extract** them from plants.

If a solution is not an acid or an alkali, we say that it is **neutral**. Neutral solutions have a pH of 7.

Alkalis have a pH above 7. Adding an acid lowers the pH.

We use neutralisation in many everyday situations. For example, we use **indigestion** tablets to neutralise some of the acid in our stomach.

An acid and an alkali **react** to cancel each other out. We call this **neutralisation**.

When an acid and an alkali react, they make a **salt** and water.

Different acids and alkalis make different salts.

Simple chemical reactions

In this unit we shall be studying some chemical reactions. We shall look at what happens when acids react with metals and when acids react with carbonates. We shall also find out more about burning.

KEY WORDS
chemical reaction
hydrogen
reactants
products
corrosion
word equation
carbonate
carbon dioxide
lime-water
oxygen
burning
combustion
oxide
fuel
explosion
fire triangle
fossil fuel

7F.1 Chemical reactions

In a **chemical reaction**, new substances are made. Chemical reactions are happening all around you. They happen in your kitchen, in your garden and inside your body. Chemical reactions break down the food that you eat into simple substances. More chemical reactions then build the simple substances up into different things like flesh and bone.

If you heat an egg, the substances in it change into new substances. Chemical reactions have happened.

The runny inside goes hard. The taste of the egg changes too.

If you heat ice, it changes to water and then to steam. Ice, water and steam are all the same chemical. You have changed it from a solid to a gas but you haven't made a new substance. So this is <u>not</u> a chemical reaction.

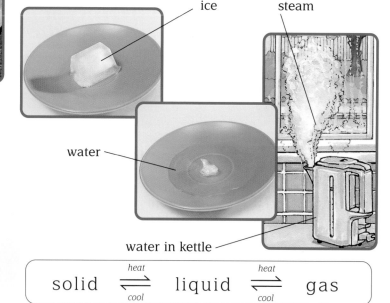
ice · steam · water · water in kettle

1 Write down an everyday example of a chemical reaction.

2 What happens in a chemical reaction?

3 Why isn't changing ice into water a chemical reaction?

$$\text{solid} \underset{cool}{\overset{heat}{\rightleftharpoons}} \text{liquid} \underset{cool}{\overset{heat}{\rightleftharpoons}} \text{gas}$$

7F.2 Reactions between acids and metals

In this topic we are going to look at what happens when you add an acid to a metal. Look at the picture.

1 Write down <u>two</u> changes that you can see.

In Olwen's first experiment, she added an acid to magnesium. Then she tested the gas given off with a lighted splint.

The 'pop' showed that the gas was **hydrogen**.

In this experiment, magnesium and hydrochloric acid <u>react</u> together. So we call them **reactants**.

Magnesium chloride and hydrogen are <u>produced</u> in the reaction. So we call them **products**.

There is less metal at the end of the reaction because it has been changed into a new substance. A word to describe the disappearance of the metal is **corrosion**.

You can describe a chemical reaction by writing a **word equation**. You write all the reactants on the left and all the products on the right. The arrow shows the direction of the reaction.

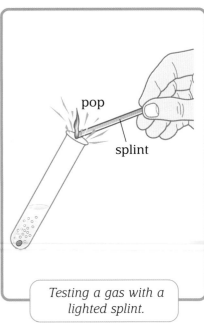

| reactants | → | products |

So the word equation for Olwen' s first experiment is:

magnesium + hydrochloric acid → magnesium chloride + hydrogen

For her second experiment, Olwen used magnesium and sulphuric acid. She tested the gas produced and found out that it was hydrogen too.

2 a What did Olwen do to test for hydrogen?

b What happened?

3 For Olwen's second experiment:

a write down the reactants **b** write down the products

c use the reactants and products to write a word equation.

4 Olwen noticed that there was less magnesium at the end of the experiment. Write down <u>one</u> word that describes the disappearance of the magnesium.

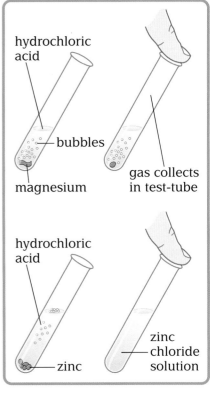

Testing a gas with a lighted splint.

7F.3 Reactions between acids and carbonates

Washing soda, baking powder and many rocks contain **carbonates**. Geologists test rocks to see if the rocks contain carbonates. If a rock fizzes when a geologist adds acid, the rock contains carbonates.

1 Write down <u>one</u> example of a carbonate.

Carbonates fizz when an acid is added to them because they give off a gas called **carbon dioxide**.

If you test carbon dioxide with a lighted splint, it does not 'pop'. The flame goes out.

2 Do carbonates fizz because of a chemical reaction? Explain your answer.

Limestone is made of calcium carbonate.

If you bubble carbon dioxide through **lime-water**, the lime-water goes cloudy.

3 Write down the gas produced when acids and carbonates react.

4 Write down <u>two</u> tests for carbon dioxide.

5 Which of the two tests do you think is the better test for carbon dioxide?

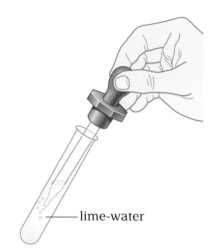

lime-water

Carbon dioxide is the only gas that makes lime-water go cloudy.

Using carbonates at home

To make light fluffy cakes we often use a mixture called 'baking powder'. The ingredients in baking powder are tartaric acid and sodium bicarbonate. They don't react when they are dry.

When tartaric acid and sodium bicarbonate react, they make carbon dioxide. The trapped bubbles get bigger as the cake cooks.

So the cake rises until it goes solid.

6 What gas does baking powder produce?

7 How does baking powder help in making cakes?

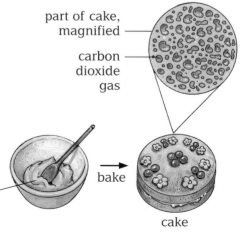

part of cake, magnified

carbon dioxide gas

bake

baking powder in the cake mix

cake

7F.4 Reactions when substances burn

Oxygen reacts with most substances. When this reaction is fast and gives out heat and light, we call it **burning** or **combustion**. When substances burn in air they react only with the oxygen in the air.

1 What gas is always used in burning?

Look at the pictures. They both show gases being burnt, but with differing results.

b Burning acetylene in oxygen.

a Burning natural gas in air.

2 Write down <u>two</u> differences between the flames.
3 Why are the two flames different?

4 Which flame do you think is the hotter? Explain your answer.
5 Why is the welder wearing eye protection in the pictures?

The general word equation for burning is:

> substance + oxygen → substance **oxide**

Many substances will burn in oxygen. You have to be careful because the reactions can produce a lot of heat and light. Also, it is dangerous to breathe in the fumes. Non-metal oxides are acidic so they can irritate your lungs.

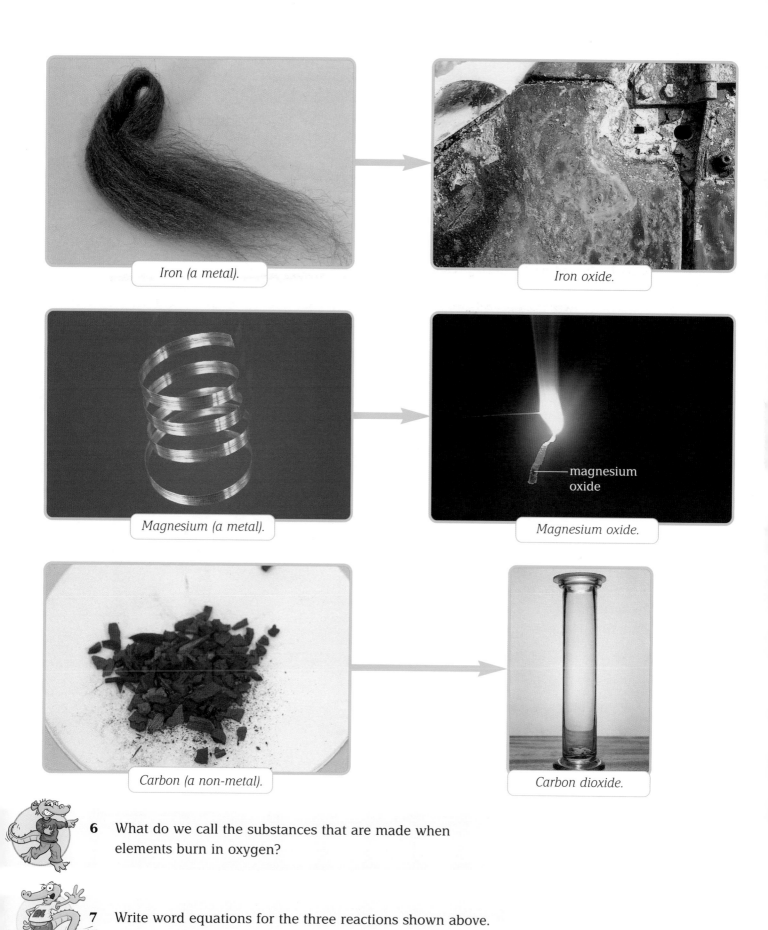

Iron (a metal).

Iron oxide.

Magnesium (a metal).

magnesium oxide

Magnesium oxide.

Carbon (a non-metal).

Carbon dioxide.

6 What do we call the substances that are made when elements burn in oxygen?

7 Write word equations for the three reactions shown above.

7F.5 Reactions when fuels burn

We burn some substances to give us the energy we need for heating and cooking. We call them **fuels**.

Hydrogen gas burns in air to form water. When hydrogen burns, lots of energy is released. If hydrogen is mixed with a lot of air, it burns very quickly and produces an **explosion**.

1 Why don't we use hydrogen as a fuel in our homes?

2 Look at the word equation.

> hydrogen + oxygen → water

Write down:

a the reactants

b the product.

Hydrogen is the lightest gas. It was once used to fill huge airships that carried passengers.

3 Find out why hydrogen airships were not used for long and why they were all dismantled.

The fire triangle

Three things are needed to make a fire. We can think of these three things as the three sides of a triangle – the **fire triangle**.

● We need oxygen from the <u>air</u>.

● We need a <u>fuel</u>.

● We need <u>heat</u> to set fire to the fuel.

Then the fuel burns to produce light and more heat.

If we take away one of these three 'sides', the fire goes out.

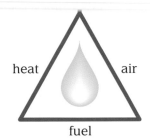

4 Write down <u>three</u> things that are needed for a fire to burn.

5 Look at the three pictures of ways of fighting fires. They all work by removing one of the three 'sides' needed for a fire. Explain how each one works.

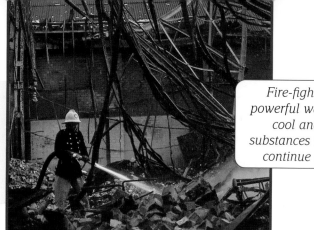

Fire-fighters use powerful water jets to cool and soak substances that might continue to burn.

Fire extinguishers often contain carbon dioxide, a heavy gas, or a foam. They smother a fire by keeping the air out.

Bulldozers can be used to remove trees in a strip.

The substances produced when fuels burn

We use a lot of energy every day for lighting, heating, cooking and entertainment, and to transport us to work or school.

Most of this energy is produced by burning **fossil fuels**. We burn fossil fuels in power stations and at home.

Natural gas, butane, oil, petrol and paraffin are fossil fuels. They contain only hydrogen and carbon. So when they burn, they produce oxides of hydrogen and carbon.

The word equation for burning a fossil fuel is:

Paraffin lamp.

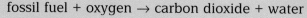
fossil fuel + oxygen → carbon dioxide + water

6 Look at the pictures. For each picture, write down the fuel used.

7 Write down the name of a gas that is

   a used in burning **b** made when a fuel burns.

8 Natural gas is also called methane. Write a word equation for what happens when methane burns.

7F.6 Looking at a candle burning

Wax is a very difficult substance to burn. It has to be turned into a gas before it will burn. Like ice, wax takes a lot of heat to melt it and then to turn it into a gas.

$$\text{solid} \xrightarrow{\text{heat}} \text{liquid} \xrightarrow{\text{heat}} \text{gas (vapour)}$$

$$\text{wax} \xrightarrow{\text{heat}} \text{molten wax} \xrightarrow{\text{heat}} \text{wax vapour}$$

- When you light a candle, the heat from the flame melts the wax.
- The wick soaks up the molten wax, in the same way that blotting paper soaks up water.
- The flame heats the small amount of liquid wax on the wick.
- This turns the liquid wax into wax vapour.
- The wax vapour mixes with air and burns.
- This produces carbon particles that glow yellow in the heat.
- As more air mixes in, the carbon also burns.

1   What does the candle use for fuel?

2   How does the fuel get to the flame?

Putting a candle out

3   Explain why blowing hard on a candle puts it out. Which side of the fire triangle is being removed?

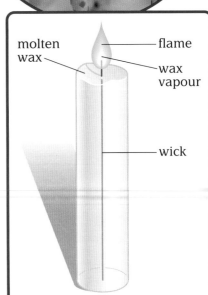

molten wax — flame
wax vapour
wick

Another way of putting a candle out

This is what happened when Ahmed put a jar over a burning candle:

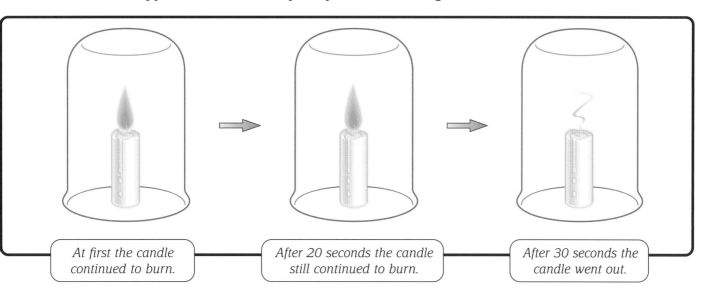

At first the candle continued to burn.	*After 20 seconds the candle still continued to burn.*	*After 30 seconds the candle went out.*

4 Describe what happens to the flame after the jar has been put over the burning candle.

5 What new substances are trapped under the jar?

6 Why do you think the candle went out? (Hint: Think about what gets used up when a candle burns.)

7 Ahmed did the experiment again, but he used a bigger jar. What difference do you think this made?

8 Look at the pie chart. Is all the air used up in burning? Explain your answer.

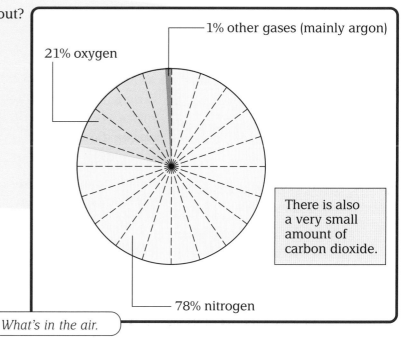

21% oxygen

1% other gases (mainly argon)

78% nitrogen

There is also a very small amount of carbon dioxide.

What's in the air.

You should now know these key words and key ideas.

Key words

chemical reaction	carbonate	oxide
hydrogen	carbon dioxide	fuel
reactants	lime-water	explosion
products	oxygen	fire triangle
corrosion	burning	fossil fuel
word equation	combustion	

Key ideas

In a **chemical reaction** new substances are produced.

Substances that are used up in a chemical reaction are called **reactants**.

Substances that are made during a chemical reaction are called **products**.

Gases are often produced in chemical reactions.

Hydrogen is produced when an acid reacts with a metal. The metal is used up. We call this **corrosion**.

We test for hydrogen using a lighted splint. You hear a 'pop' if there is hydrogen.

We can describe a chemical reaction with a **word equation**.

An acid reacts with a **carbonate** to produce new substances. One of these is **carbon dioxide**.

We use **lime-water** to test for carbon dioxide. It is the only gas that turns lime-water cloudy.

Oxygen reacting with a substance is called **burning** or **combustion**.

The **oxide** of a substance is made when a substance burns.

Fuels release energy when they burn.

An **explosion** is very fast burning.

A fire needs oxygen from air, fuel and heat to burn. We show this as a **fire triangle**.

Fossil fuels contain only carbon and hydrogen. They release carbon dioxide and water when they burn.

Particle model: solids, liquids and gases

In this unit we shall look at the way our ideas about substances have changed. We shall also learn how to use these ideas to explain things that we see in laboratory experiments and in everyday life.

KEY WORDS
matter
material
substance
evidence
theory
model
particle
solid
liquid
gas
states of matter
flow
Brownian motion
random
particle model of matter
kinetic theory
vibrate
compress
diffusion
pressure
expansion
heat conduction

7G.1 Looking at and thinking about substances

All the stuff we see and feel in the world we call **matter** or **material**. Types of matter are called **substances**. Substances include water, gold, leaves, brick, hair and acids. There are millions of different types of substances.

1 Write down the names of <u>ten</u> substances that are part of the matter in the room with you now.

You can study substances in lots of different ways. You can do experiments with substances to see what they do. You might be surprised how some substances behave.

2 Look at the pictures. Choose <u>one</u> of the experiments shown in the pictures. Write down your idea to explain what you see.

When you do experiments, you write down observations and measurements. All of the observations and measurements are called **evidence**. You can use evidence to help you to explain things. Scientists work in this way too.

You can smell the gas given off by the air freshener

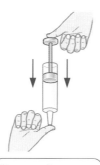

Some substances can be squashed

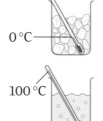

0 °C
100 °C

Some substances get bigger when you heat them

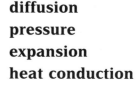

190.0 g
003.6 g
024.3 g

Some substances are heavier than others

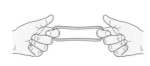

Some substances get longer

3 Write down <u>two</u> things that scientists do to collect evidence.

4 a Imagine using a very powerful microscope to look inside the substance that you chose in question 2. What do you think it is like inside? Discuss your ideas with another pupil.

b If you have changed your mind about your answer to question 2, write down your new idea. Don't cross out the old idea.

7G.2 Thinking about theories

Some scientists collect evidence about matter. They use their imaginations to think of ideas to explain the evidence. We call these ideas **theories**. Sometimes scientists make pictures in their minds as part of their theory.

1 What is a theory?

Scientists discuss their theories and argue about them. They don't always agree. The scientists often need to look for more evidence. Then they try to see if their theory also explains the new evidence. If it doesn't, they change their theory, or even make a new theory altogether. When they think that a theory explains all the evidence, the group of ideas and pictures in their imagination is called a **model**.

2 What do scientists call theories that explain all the evidence?

3 Why do you think scientists argue about their ideas?

Scientists discuss and argue about ideas all the time.

Making a theory is very similar to what happens as a detective tries to solve a crime. The detective collects clues. She makes up theories, and discusses and argues with other detectives. She looks for more clues. When she finds more clues, she may change her theory. She keeps doing this until the evidence can be explained and the criminal is caught.

4 How is the work of a detective like that of a scientist? Make a list of the things that are the same.

A theory about matter

We call very small pieces of matter **particles**. The idea that matter is made of very small particles is very old. Over 2000 years ago in ancient Greece, a scientist called Democritus said that everything was made of small particles.

To explain what he meant, Democritus asked people to imagine that he had a bar of gold and a magic knife. The magic knife could cut any substance. When he cut the bar of gold in half, the two halves were smaller than the whole bar. As he kept cutting, the pieces got smaller and smaller. After many cuts, he would get a very small particle that the knife would not cut.

Democritus believed that everything could be cut this way and that all matter is made of particles. He argued with other thinkers. Some agreed with him but others did not.

Democritus.

5 Write a letter to a relative about Democritus and his particle idea. Say whether or not you agree with Democritus's theory, and why.

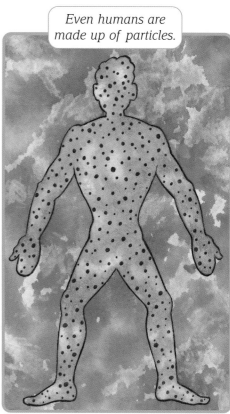

Even humans are made up of particles.

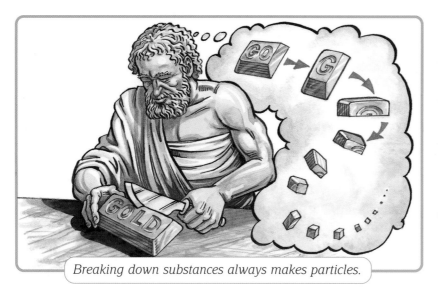

Breaking down substances always makes particles.

7G.3 A closer look at solids, liquids and gases

You probably know how important grouping and sorting is in everyday life! To make it easier to study and understand the world, scientists also sort things into groups.
For example, scientists divide living things into two groups: plants and animals. Then they divide these very large groups into other smaller groups.

Another way that scientists use to sort substances is to group them into **solids**, **liquids** and **gases**. Scientists call these three groups the three **states of matter**.

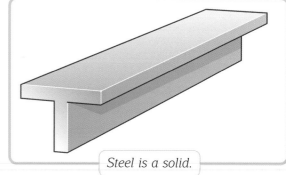

Steel is a solid.

1 Write down the three states of matter.

Solids have a definite shape and volume. They are very difficult to squash. Some solids seem to be heavy for their size. Steel is hard.

2 A man jumps up and down on a large stone.
Does the stone change shape?

Liquids take up the shape of the container they are in and keep the same volume. They are difficult to squash. Liquids can **flow**, which means they can be poured and can move through gaps. Generally, liquids aren't very heavy for their size.

Water is a liquid.

3 Water can be poured easily, but ice cannot.
What states of matter do water and ice belong to?

4 Milk is poured from a bottle into a jug. Does the shape of the milk change?

Gases fill any container. Gases flow like liquids. They are very easy to squash. Most gases are light for their size.

5 Water and gas come through pipes into houses. Why can both water and gas be delivered in this way?

Nitrogen dioxide is a brown gas.

6 Write down <u>three</u> properties of:

a solids **b** liquids **c** gases.

7G.4 Some evidence for the particle theory

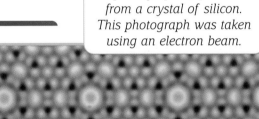

A photograph of particles from a crystal of silicon. This photograph was taken using an electron beam.

You read about Democritus's theory about particles on page 79. Lots of people discussed his theory and argued about it. The problem was that evidence was hard to find. Eventually the idea of particles was forgotten for hundreds of years.

But now, the idea of particles is widely accepted by scientists. Many scientists collected evidence over many years. Now scientists can even take photographs of particles using X-rays and electron beams. The particles are very, very small; they are much too small for us to see in any other way.

1 What new techniques gave scientists direct evidence for particles?

2 What can you say about the size of particles in the air?

Robert Brown and small moving things

In 1827, a Scottish biologist called Robert Brown used a microscope to look at pollen grains in water. The pollen grains jiggled around and followed a zigzag path. He thought that pollen grains were living, moving creatures. What was very strange was that 100-year-old pollen grains did the same jiggling. Scientists called this type of movement **Brownian motion**. They kept discussing whether the pollen was alive or dead.

Robert Brown (1773–1858).

Some scientists looked at other substances, such as smoke, dust, soot grains and scrapings of pencil leads. These scientists also saw Brownian motion. The small bits these scientist looked at could not be alive. So, scientists had to make up a new theory to explain Brownian motion.

3 Eventually, scientists agreed that pollen grains weren't alive even though they were moving. Write down <u>one</u> piece of evidence that they used to support this idea.

In 1877, a French scientist called Desaulx argued that very small, invisible air particles moving in a random way caused Brownian motion. **Random** means you can't tell which way something will move next. Look at the picture to see what Desaulx meant.

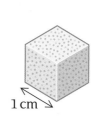

A 1 cm³ cube of air contains about 30 million million million particles (30 × 10¹⁸).

The path of a pollen grain that is jiggling about.

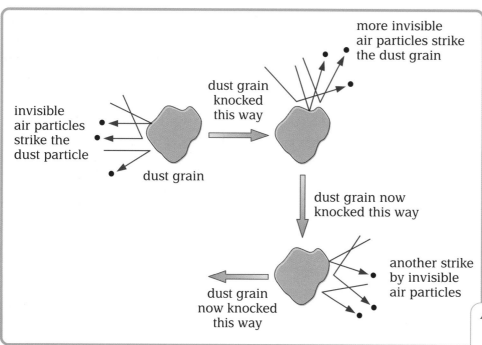

A dust grain is hit by invisible air particles, making it jiggle about in a random way.

4 What did Desaulx think caused Brownian motion?

In 1900, another scientist, F. M. Exner, found that smaller granules moved faster. He also showed that they moved faster when they were warmer. In 1905, Albert Einstein calculated the sizes and speeds of the particles at different temperatures. He used mathematics to draw exact charts of Brownian motion. This work was part of the reason he won the 1921 Nobel Prize for Physics.

5 What happens to the movement of particles as the temperature rises?

6 Did Exner's discoveries provide evidence for either of the two theories about Brownian motion? Explain your answer.

7 It is a bright sunny day. In a boy's bedroom, the sun shines through a gap in the curtains. The boy sees dust particles in the strong beam of light. The bits of dust seem to jiggle around even though there is no wind. Try to explain what is happening to the bits of dust.

We can see how Brown, Desaulx, Exner and Einstein developed Democritus's theory about particles. They gathered evidence and suggested theories. They changed their theories when they found new evidence.

The theory changed until it had five main ideas. These five ideas are called the **particle model of matter**.

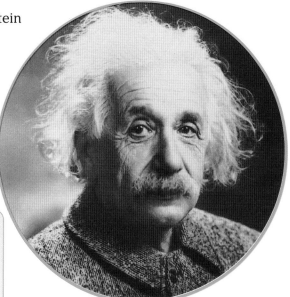

Albert Einstein (1879–1955). He proved that the particle model of matter explained Brownian motion.

1 All matter is made up of particles.

2 The particles can be of different sizes.

3 The particles move around by themselves in a random way.

4 The particles attract each other.

5 The hotter the substance, the faster the particles move.

Some scientists call this model the **kinetic theory**. <u>Kinetic</u> is the Greek word for <u>movement</u> (scientists often use Greek words).

8 Pretend you are writing an email, back through time, to Robert Brown. Explain why you think pollen grains are not living creatures even though they jiggle around when you look at them under a microscope. You need to mention the particle model of matter in your email.

7G.5 Using the particle model

In this topic we will see how the particle model can explain many of the observations we have made about matter.

Particles in crystals

Many solids are made up of crystals. Crystals have straight edges.

Look at the straight edges of these crystals.

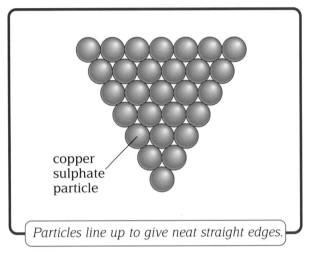

copper sulphate particle

Particles line up to give neat straight edges.

1 Write down the names of two crystals.

2 Do all the crystals have sharp, straight edges?

3 Use the particle model to explain why both small and large crystals of the same substance have the same shape.

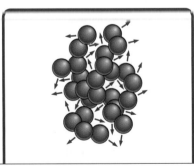

In solids, the particles vibrate while staying in their places.

Particles in solids, liquids and gases

Solids, liquids and gases are all made up of particles.

In solids, forces of attraction hold the particles together. The particles **vibrate** but they don't change place with the particles next to them. Vibrate means to move from side to side. There is very little space between the particles.

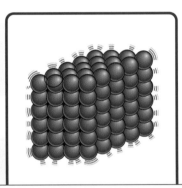

In liquids, the particles still vibrate. They are attracted to each other less than in a solid. This means they can swap places with each other.

4 Write down two differences between the particles in a solid and a liquid.

5 Liquids take the shape of their containers and they can be poured. Use the particle model to explain these properties.

In a gas the particles are far apart and are moving very fast. There is very little attraction between the particles and they move about freely.

6 In which one of solids, liquids and gases:

　a are the particles closest together?

　b is the attraction between particles the greatest?

　c can particles move about the most freely?

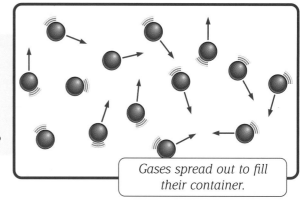

Gases spread out to fill their container.

Compressing solids, liquids and gases

The scientific word for 'squashing' is **compressing**. Solids and liquids are difficult to compress. Gases are easy to compress. We can use the particle model to explain these differences.

7 Explain why gases are easy to compress, but liquids and solids are not.

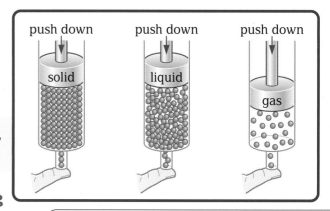

Only gases have enough space between their particles for the particles to be squeezed together.

Melting, boiling, freezing and condensing

We use heat to melt a solid. Heat makes the particles move faster. When the particles get enough energy, they start to overcome the attractive forces between them. The particles can then start to swap places – the solid melts to form a liquid.

If we continue to heat the particles, they get even more energy and move faster still. Spaces open up between the particles until a gas is formed. The liquid has boiled.

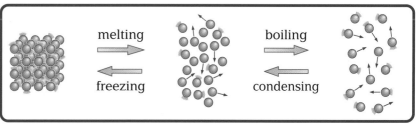

Condensing is the reverse of boiling. Freezing is the reverse of melting.

8 When you heat up a solid, what happens to the particles?

9 When you cool a gas, what happens to the speed of the particles?

Diffusion

Look at the pictures. They show how some substances seem to spread out without any help from air currents, water currents or stirring. We call this spreading out **diffusion**.

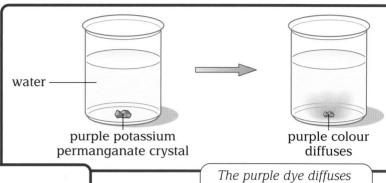

water —

purple potassium permanganate crystal

purple colour diffuses

The purple dye diffuses through the water.

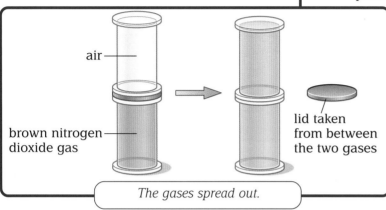

air —

brown nitrogen dioxide gas

lid taken from between the two gases

The gases spread out.

10 What is diffusion?

11 Look at the pictures. Write down <u>one</u> example of diffusion of:

   a a gas   **b** a dissolved solid.

12 Look at the pictures of the particles in the brown gas and the air. Describe what happens when you remove the lid between the two gases.

We can use the particle model to explain diffusion

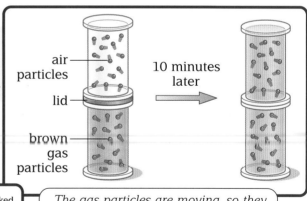

air particles

lid

10 minutes later

brown gas particles

The gas particles are moving, so they mix. We say that they diffuse.

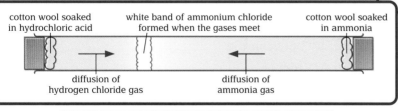

cotton wool soaked in hydrochloric acid

white band of ammonium chloride formed when the gases meet

cotton wool soaked in ammonia

diffusion of hydrogen chloride gas

diffusion of ammonia gas

The two transparent gases diffuse. They form a white cloud when they meet. Both of the gases have particles that are moving.

13 Use the particle model to explain what is happening in the glass tube.

14 A girl is doing some cooking in the kitchen. The cooking smells soon reach her brother's room. He calls down to ask what she is cooking. Explain <u>one</u> way that the smell could have got up to her brother's room.

15 A balloon full of air goes down slowly, even though the knot at the bottom of the balloon is airtight. After a week all the air has escaped from the balloon. Use the particle model to explain why this happens. Write down what you think. Draw a diagram to help explain how the air particles got out of the balloon.

The can crushing experiment

Peter heated a can containing a little water. The water boiled and the steam drove out most of the air from inside the can. Peter screwed the lid back on the can and left it to cool. As the can cooled it collapsed.

The particle model can help us to explain what happens in Peter's experiment. The steam forces out the air particles that were inside the can. As the steam cools, it turns back to water. The can now has mainly liquid water inside it.

This means that there are more air particles hitting the outside of the can than are hitting the inside. The outside air particles batter the can inwards and crush it. The **pressure** or pushing force of the particles on the outside of the can is greater than the pressure on the inside.

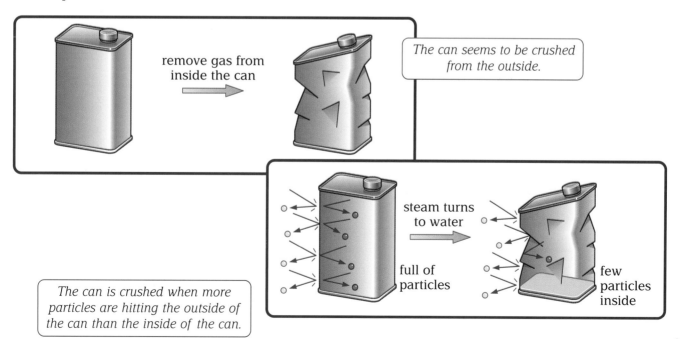

remove gas from inside the can

The can seems to be crushed from the outside.

steam turns to water

full of particles

few particles inside

The can is crushed when more particles are hitting the outside of the can than the inside of the can.

7G.6 More uses of the particle model

Liquids and gases flow but solids don't

In solids, the forces of attraction between the particles are too big to allow the rows of particles to break up and flow. In liquids, the forces are smaller and so they can flow when they are poured. In gases, the attractive forces between particles are slight. Gas particles can flow out of a beaker without the beaker even being tipped up.

1   What is the difference in the forces between the particles in solids, in liquids and in gases?

2   Explain why solids cannot flow.

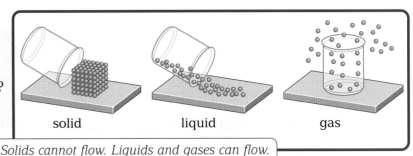

solid   liquid   gas

Solids cannot flow. Liquids and gases can flow.

Expansion and particles

Expansion means getting bigger. Most substances expand when you heat them. Solids expand slightly, liquids expand more, and gases expand a lot.

3   Which type of substance expands the most: a solid, a liquid or a gas?

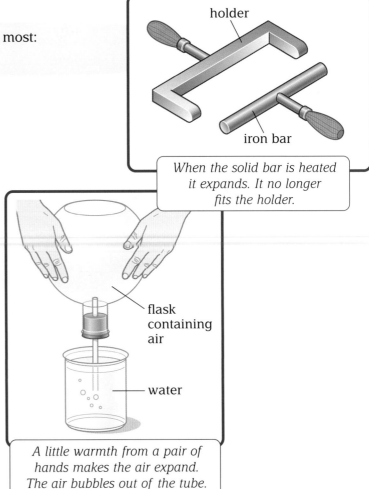

holder

iron bar

When the solid bar is heated it expands. It no longer fits the holder.

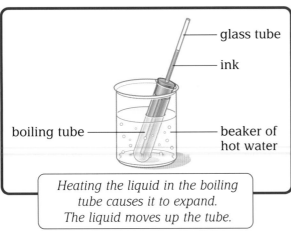

glass tube

ink

boiling tube   beaker of hot water

Heating the liquid in the boiling tube causes it to expand. The liquid moves up the tube.

flask containing air

water

When a substance expands, the particles do <u>not</u> get bigger. Instead, the particles speed up and move further apart, so they take up more space. The attractive forces between the particles are smaller in gases and liquids, so gases and liquids expand more than solids.

A little warmth from a pair of hands makes the air expand. The air bubbles out of the tube.

4 What happens to the particles when a substance expands?

5 Using the particle model, try to explain why a gas expands more than a solid. Use diagrams to help you.

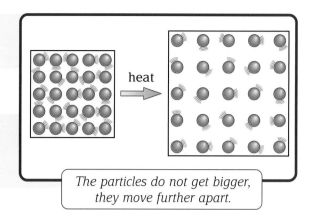

heat

The particles do not get bigger, they move further apart.

Heat conduction in solids

Look at the picture. The spoon gets hot because heat from the coffee travels through the metal of the spoon. We say that heat is conducted through the spoon.

Particles at high temperatures move and vibrate faster than those at lower temperatures. The fast vibrating particles collide and hit their slower neighbours, making these vibrate faster too. The faster vibrations pass up the metal in the spoon and eventually the top of the spoon gets hot. **Heat conduction** has taken place.

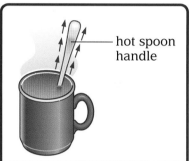

hot spoon handle

The top of the spoon gets hot.

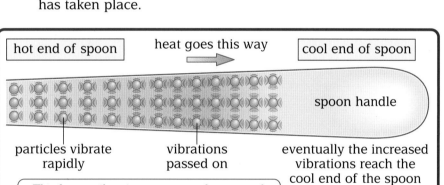

hot end of spoon — heat goes this way — cool end of spoon

spoon handle

particles vibrate rapidly

vibrations passed on

eventually the increased vibrations reach the cool end of the spoon

The faster vibrations pass up the spoon by collision. Heat travels through the metal.

6 What do we call the way heat travels through a solid?

7 Write down <u>three</u> other examples of heat conduction in solids. Describe how the particle model explains what happens in your examples.

You should now understand the key words and key ideas shown below.

When scientists have collected **evidence** they try and make pictures in their minds. They use their imaginations and make up lists of ideas that might explain the evidence. We call this making theories. When a **theory** can explain the evidence, the group of ideas and pictures is called a **model**.

We often describe **matter** or **materials** as **substances**.

The **particle model of matter**

1 All matter is made up of **particles**.
2 The particles can be of different sizes.
3 The particles move around by themselves in a **random** way.
4 The particles attract each other.
5 The hotter the substance the faster the particles move.

Some scientists call this model the **kinetic theory**.

Random movement of particles causes spreading out of particles. We call this **diffusion**.

Random movement of particles is called **Brownian motion**.

Movement of particles produces a pushing force or **pressure** on a surface.

Expansion means getting bigger. Solids expand slightly; liquids expand more and gases expand a great deal. During expansion the particles move further apart. The particles don't get bigger.

Substances can be sorted into three groups: **solids**, **liquids** and **gases**. These three groups are called the three **states of matter**.

Solids don't **flow** because the forces between the particles are strong. Gases and liquids flow because the forces between particles are much weaker.

Solids and liquids are difficult to **compress**, but gases compress easily. This is because gases have large gaps between the particles.

In **solids**, strong forces hold the particles together so they **vibrate**, but do not change places. There is little space between particles.

In **liquids**, the particles are still attracted to each other but they move faster. They swap places with each other. There is a little more space between the particles.

In a **gas**, there is little attraction between the particles so they move freely. The particles are far apart and moving very fast.

Heat travels in solids by **conduction**. The vibration of the particles is passed through a solid as the particles knock into each other.

Solutions

In this unit we shall be learning about solutions. We shall explore which solids and liquids make solutions and we will see how we can separate solids and liquids from solutions.

KEY WORDS
mixture
dissolve
solution
solute
solvent
soluble
insoluble
pure
filtration
evaporation
sodium chloride
particles
condensation
condenser
distillation
chromatography
attracted
chromatogram
saturated solution
solubility

7H.1 Mixing solids and liquids

If you have you ever spilt water on your exercise book during a science experiment you may have noticed something strange happen. The ink from your pen may 'run' but the pencil doesn't. This is because the water dissolves the ink but does not dissolve the pencil. You can see this in the picture.

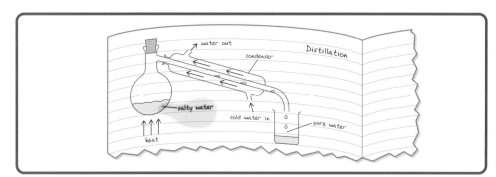

Making solutions

If you mix salt into a beaker of water the salt seems to 'vanish'. Sand just sinks to the bottom.

Both the beakers now contain **mixtures** of a solid and a liquid. However, there is one important difference. The salt **dissolves** in the water but the sand doesn't.

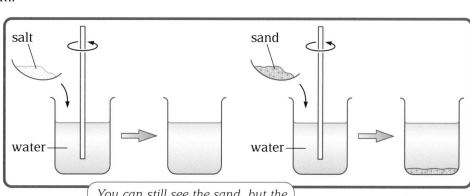

You can still see the sand, but the salt seems to have vanished.

When the salt dissolves in the water it makes a **solution**. In the salt solution the salt and water are given special names:

- the salt is called the **solute** – it is the solid that dissolves to make the solution;
- the water is called the **solvent** – it is the liquid that dissolves the salt.

The salt dissolves in water. We say that salt is **soluble** in water. When a solid dissolves it is called soluble. Sand does not dissolve in water. We say that sand is **insoluble** in water. When a solid will not dissolve it is called insoluble.

1 Write down the name of the solute and the solvent used to make a salt solution.

2 Some chalk is mixed with water. How can you tell if the chalk is soluble or insoluble?

3 If sand were soluble in water, what would happen to the world's beaches?

Everyday mixtures

A bottle of mineral water is labelled 'pure' to tell us that nothing has been added to it. However, this 'pure' mineral water contains many different minerals dissolved in water and is really a mixture. To a scientist something is **pure** only when it contains just a single substance and not a mixture of substances.

Mixtures are found everywhere. Here are some mixtures you may come across:

- mineral water is a mixture of water and dissolved minerals;
- a cup of coffee is a mixture of hot water, milk and dissolved coffee (and possibly sugar);
- milk is mainly a mixture of water, sugar, protein and fat;
- sea water is mainly a mixture of water and dissolved salt.

4 Look at the picture of the everyday mixtures. Name <u>two</u> mixtures found in the kitchen.

5 Which of the following are mixtures?

a sugar; **b** a cup of tea; **c** pure water.

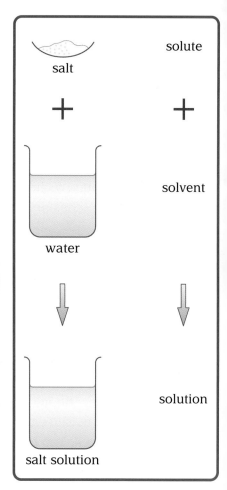

salt — solute

+ +

water — solvent

salt solution — solution

mineral water

cup of coffee

bottle of milk

sea water

Separating mixtures of solids and liquids

We have seen how you can make two completely different mixtures of solids in liquids:

● a mixture of sand and water; ● a salt solution.

We use different ways to get the solids back from both of these mixtures. We say that we use different <u>separation techniques</u>. The separation technique we use depends on whether the solid has dissolved or not.

First let's look at the sand and water mixture. The sand is insoluble and has not dissolved in the water. The sand is separated from the water using **filtration**.

Now let's look at the salt solution. The salt is soluble and has dissolved in the water. Filtering won't work because the salt solution will just go straight through the filter paper. Instead, the salt is separated from the water by **evaporation**.

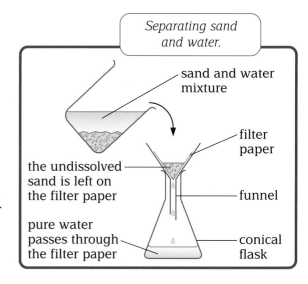

Separating sand and water.

sand and water mixture

filter paper

the undissolved sand is left on the filter paper

funnel

pure water passes through the filter paper

conical flask

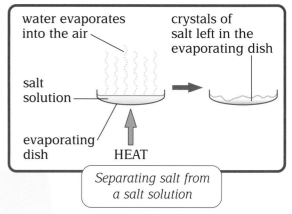

water evaporates into the air

crystals of salt left in the evaporating dish

salt solution

evaporating dish

HEAT

Separating salt from a salt solution

6 Name the separation technique used to separate:

a sand from a mixture of sand and water;

b salt from a salt solution.

7 Look at the label found on a bottle of mineral water.

a Name <u>one</u> substance dissolved in the mineral water.

b Describe how you could prove that the mineral water contains dissolved substances.

8 We use many different separation techniques in cooking. Describe <u>three</u> situations in cooking that use different separation techniques.

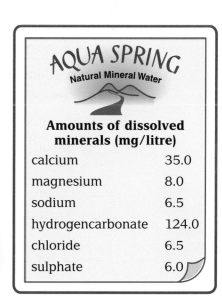

AQUA SPRING
Natural Mineral Water

Amounts of dissolved minerals (mg/litre)

calcium	35.0
magnesium	8.0
sodium	6.5
hydrogencarbonate	124.0
chloride	6.5
sulphate	6.0

7H.2 Salt of the Earth

The chemical name for salt is **sodium chloride**. Sodium chloride is often called 'common salt'. There are two main places where people find salt:

- There is a type of rock that contains a large amount of salt. This is called <u>rock salt</u>.

- There is salt in sea water.

Different countries use different methods to get common salt.

Crushed rock salt.

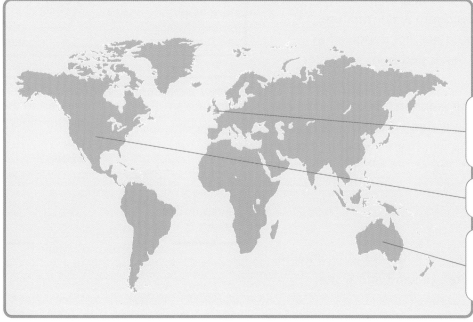

In the UK, water is pumped into the rock salt. The salt dissolves and the salt solution is pumped to the surface.

In the USA, rock salt is mined by cutting, drilling and blasting.

In Australia, sea water is collected. Sunlight is used to evaporate the water until salt crystals form.

1 What is the chemical name for 'common salt'?

2 In Australia, salt is obtained by the crystallisation of sea water. Why isn't this method used in the UK?

We spend a lot of money extracting salt. This is because both salt and rock salt have a variety of uses.

3 Write down <u>one</u> use of rock salt.

4 Write down <u>one</u> use of sodium chloride.

5 Sodium chloride is an important part of our diet. Try to find out why our bodies need sodium chloride.

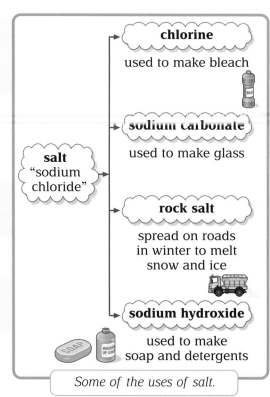

chlorine
used to make bleach

sodium carbonate
used to make glass

salt
"sodium chloride"

rock salt
spread on roads in winter to melt snow and ice

sodium hydroxide
used to make soap and detergents

Some of the uses of salt.

7H.3 The mystery of the disappearing solute!

When we dissolve salt in water, we make a colourless solution. Although the salt seems to 'vanish', it is still there. The salt reappears when the water is evaporated away. We need to explain how the salt can seem to 'vanish'.

Balanced solutions

The biggest clue to what happens to the salt when we make a solution comes from weighing. We can weigh the salt and water separately before making a solution. We can then weigh the solution that we have made.

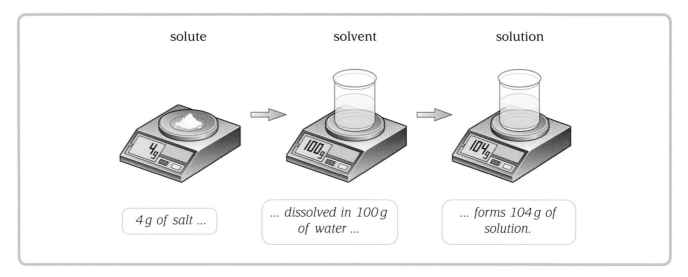

solute   solvent   solution

4 g of salt ...   ... dissolved in 100 g of water ...   ... forms 104 g of solution.

This is true for every solution: the mass of a solution always equals the total mass of the solute and the solvent. We can write this as an equation:

mass of solute + mass of solvent = mass of solution

This tells us that when a solute dissolves it hasn't really 'vanished'. It is part of the solution, so no mass is lost. This is called <u>conservation of mass</u>.

1   What mass of salt solution is made from 7 g of salt and 40 g of water?

2   What mass of salt must be added to 100 g of water to make a salt solution with a mass of 105 g?

A closer look at solutions

To explain why the solute seems to 'vanish' when we make a solution, we need to use the idea of **particles**.

When a solute dissolves it breaks apart into its individual particles. The solute and solvent particles mix together and become totally mixed up. That's why a solution is a mixture! As the solute and solvent particles become mixed up, no matter is lost. The overall mass stays the same.

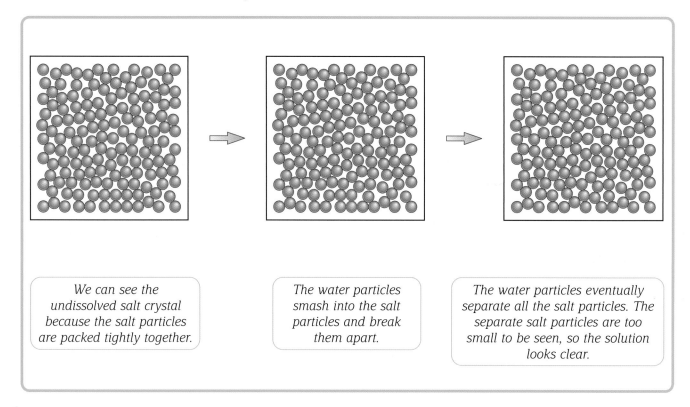

We can see the undissolved salt crystal because the salt particles are packed tightly together.

The water particles smash into the salt particles and break them apart.

The water particles eventually separate all the salt particles. The separate salt particles are too small to be seen, so the solution looks clear.

3 How do the solvent particles break up the solute?

4 Describe how the solute and solvent particles are arranged in a solution.

5 10 g of salt is dissolved in 100 g of water. Use the idea of particles to explain why the mass of the salt solution is 110 g.

6 Why is it not possible to get the salt out of a salt solution using filtration? You need to think about:

- how the salt and water particles are arranged in a solution;
- the size of the salt and water particles and the size of the 'holes' in filter paper.

7H.4 Separating solvents from solutes

We have already seen how to get the solute back from a solution. When we heat a salt solution, the water evaporates and leaves the salt behind. We now need to find a way to collect the water.

The separation and collection of water from a solution is important if we want to be able to purify water. It is often important in chemistry experiments to use extremely pure water that contains no dissolved impurities. This pure water is called <u>distilled water</u>. The name 'distilled water' gives us a big clue to how the water has been purified.

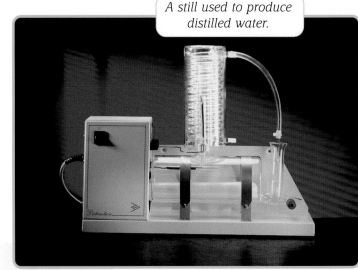

A still used to produce distilled water.

1   What is the name of the pure water used in some chemistry experiments?

2   Why is it important sometimes to use pure water?

Getting the solvent back – distillation

You may have noticed that bathroom mirrors steam up when you have a hot bath. The hot steam from the bath hits the cold mirror. The cold mirror cools the steam back into water. This is called **condensation**.

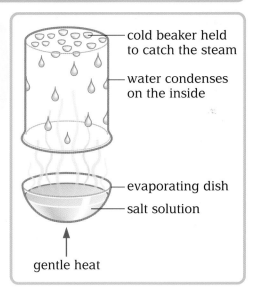

Everyday condensation.

3   Why does the steam change into water when it hits the mirror?

4   What is the process called when steam changes back into water?

It is the idea that steam changes back into water when the steam hits a cold surface that helps us separate water from a salt solution.

When a salt solution is heated up the water evaporates as steam. The water changes state from a liquid to a gas. The steam can be condensed back into pure water by cooling it down. The steam changes state from a gas back into a liquid. All we need now is a way to collect the water.

cold beaker held to catch the steam

water condenses on the inside

evaporating dish

salt solution

gentle heat

5 Describe the changes of state that occur during:

a evaporation;

b condensation.

The water is collected using a **condenser**. This whole process is called **distillation**.

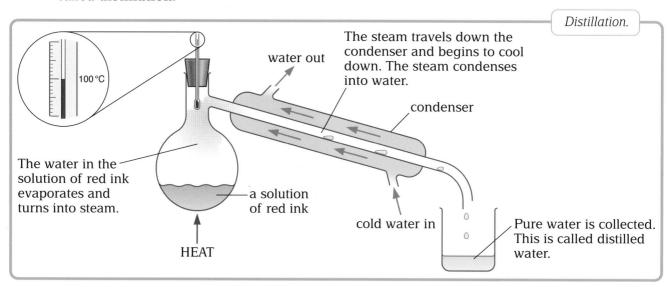

Distillation.

The water in the solution of red ink evaporates and turns into steam.

100 °C

water out

The steam travels down the condenser and begins to cool down. The steam condenses into water.

condenser

a solution of red ink

cold water in

HEAT

Pure water is collected. This is called distilled water.

Distillation is the process in which the evaporation of a liquid is followed by its condensation:

● evaporation – the liquid solvent changes to a gas as it is heated up;

● condensation – the gas changes back into a liquid as it is cooled down.

During distillation the solute doesn't evaporate, so the solute is left behind in the flask.

6 What is the temperature reading on the thermometer?

7 Explain why the thermometer shows this temperature.

8 The condenser is named after a German scientist who believed in using practical work to teach chemistry. Try to find out the name of this scientist and any other contributions he made to chemistry.

7H.5 Chromatography

Some solutions contain a mixture of different solutes. The technique used to separate a mixture of two or more solutes is called **chromatography**.

This diagram shows one method you can use to do chromatography in a school laboratory.

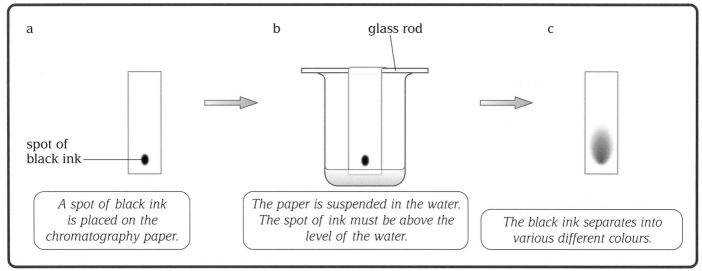

a

spot of black ink —

A spot of black ink is placed on the chromatography paper.

b

glass rod

The paper is suspended in the water. The spot of ink must be above the level of the water.

c

The black ink separates into various different colours.

1 Black ink is a mixture. Look at these diagrams. Which colours of ink are mixed to make the black ink?

2 What is this method of separation called?

*The piece of chromatography paper shows how the parts of the mixture have been separated. The piece of paper is called a **chromatogram**.*

3 Why mustn't the spot of black ink be placed in the water?

Water is a solvent for the ink. As the water is soaked up by the filter paper the water dissolves the ink. As the water spreads out it carries the ink with it. The ink particles are **attracted** to the water particles. The water particles move the particles of ink by giving them 'piggyback rides'.

The more firmly an ink particle attaches itself to a water particle the further it will be carried in a given amount of time.

4 What is the result of chromatography called?

The black ink is a mixture of yellow, red, brown and blue inks. The yellow ink has been carried the furthest. So, the yellow ink is the most soluble in water. The blue ink has been carried the least. So the blue ink is the least soluble in water.

Chromatography only works if the test mixture is soluble in the solvent. For example, not all paints are soluble in water. So, we need to use a different solvent, such as white spirit, that will dissolve the paint.

5 A sample of blue paint doesn't dissolve in water. How would you carry out chromatography on this paint?

Making use of chromatography

One possible use of chromatography is to study food dyes. Some foods are coloured using a mixture of food dyes. You may want to find out which food dyes have been used in a particular food if you are allergic to one food dye.

We can use chromatography to find out how many different food dyes are used to make the coloured coatings on chocolate sweets.

This chromatogram shows that the blue and yellow food colourings are pure, but the brown food colouring is a mixture of red, yellow and blue.

6 How many different dyes does Food Colouring 1 contain?

7 Name the dyes found in Food Colouring 2.

8 Which dye is the most soluble?

9 You have an allergic reaction to Food Colouring 2 but not Food Colouring 1. Which food dye are you allergic to?

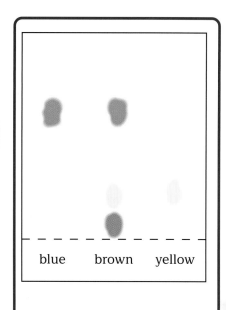

blue   brown   yellow

Chromatography results for blue, brown and yellow food colourings.

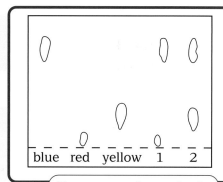

blue red yellow 1 2

Chromatography results for blue, red and yellow food dyes and two different food colourings.

More uses of chromatography

Scientists use chromatography to help them in a wide range of situations. These include:

- biology, for example finding out which pigments are contained in leaves;

- forensic science, for example comparing the blood of a suspect with blood found at the scene of a crime;

- medicine, for example testing urine to identify traces of substances in it to check a patient's health.

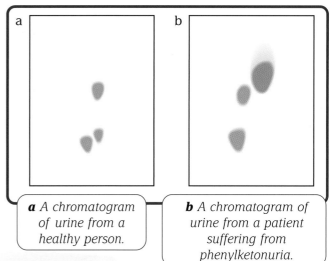

a A chromatogram of urine from a healthy person.

b A chromatogram of urine from a patient suffering from phenylketonuria.

10 Two cars were involved in an accident. One driver drove off without stopping. However, some red paint was left behind on the other car. The police have three suspects, each owning red cars. Describe how they could use chromatography to prove which red car was involved in the accident.

7H.6 Solubility

If we keep adding salt to water at room temperature there comes a point when no more salt will dissolve. However hard we try, there is a limit to the amount of solid that dissolves in a particular volume of water. A solution where no more solid will dissolve is called a **saturated solution**.

1 What happens to salt that is added to a saturated solution?

2 How can you tell that a salt solution is saturated?

Solubility

We already know that some solids are soluble in water whilst others are insoluble. In fact, different solids are soluble in different amounts. For example, sodium chloride is very soluble and dissolves easily in water, but lead chloride is only slightly soluble and is quite hard to dissolve in water.

Solubility is a measure of how soluble something is. The higher its solubility the more soluble it is.

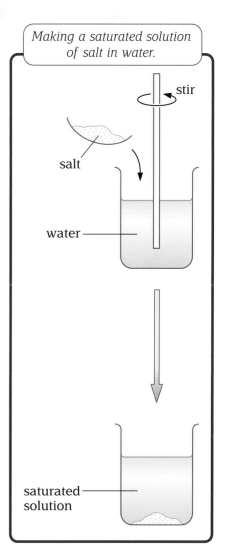

Making a saturated solution of salt in water.

stir

salt

water

saturated solution

To compare the solubility of different solutes we need to make the comparison fair. To do this we measure the maximum mass of a solute that will dissolve in 100 g of the solvent. In effect, what we are doing is starting with 100 g of a solvent and measuring how much solute we can dissolve until we make a saturated solution.

Substance	Solubility in grams per 100 g of water
calcium chloride	74
copper sulphate	21
potassium chlorate	7
potassium nitrate	300
sand	0
sodium chloride	36

3 What do we call the measure of how soluble something is?

4 Look at the table. Which substance is the most soluble in water?

5 Which substance is insoluble in water? Explain your answer.

Changing the solvent

Imagine you have spilt some oil on your shirt. You have to buy a special stain remover to remove the oil. The stain remover does this because it contains a solvent that dissolves the oil.

If we want to dissolve a solid we have to select the solvent very carefully. This means that we must name the solvent when solubility is stated. For example, sodium chloride has a solubility of 36 g in 100 g <u>of water</u>.

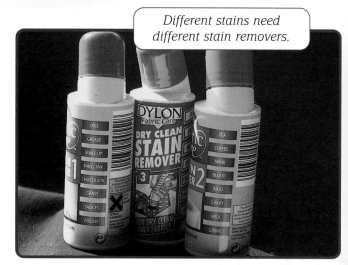

Different stains need different stain removers.

6 Name <u>one</u> substance that doesn't dissolve in water.

7 Why must the solvent be named when solubility is stated?

8 Different stain removers are designed to remove different stains. How can they do this?

Temperature and solubility

You may have noticed that sugar is easy to dissolve in a cup of hot tea, but not so easy to dissolve if the tea is cooler.

For many solutes their solubility increases as the temperature increases. This means that more solute will dissolve in a warm solvent than in a cold solvent. It is important that the temperature is given when solubility is stated. For example, sodium chloride has a solubility of 36 g in 100 g of water <u>at 20 °C</u>.

When we compare the solubility of different solutes, we often need to do so for a range of temperatures.

A good way of showing how solubility changes as the temperature changes is to plot the data as a graph.

The graph here shows that the solubility of all three solids increases as the temperature increases. The curves can be used to work out the solubility of any of the solids at any temperature. For example, we can see that the solubility of copper sulphate in 100 g of water at 80 °C is 55 g. Having the three curves on the same graph also lets us compare the solubility of the three solids.

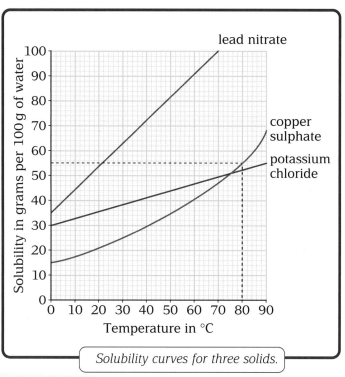

Solubility curves for three solids.

9 What happens to the solubility of all three solids as the temperature increases?

10 What is the solubility of lead nitrate at 60 °C?

11 Which solid is the most soluble at 10 °C?

12 At what temperature are the solubilities of potassium chloride and copper sulphate the same?

13 The solubility of which solid is most affected by temperature?

14 Rob made a cup of coffee using coffee granules in a mug of hot water. Unfortunately, Rob forgot about the coffee. The next day he found that there was solid coffee in the bottom of the mug. Use the ideas of solubility and saturated solutions to explain this.

You should now understand the key words and key ideas shown below.

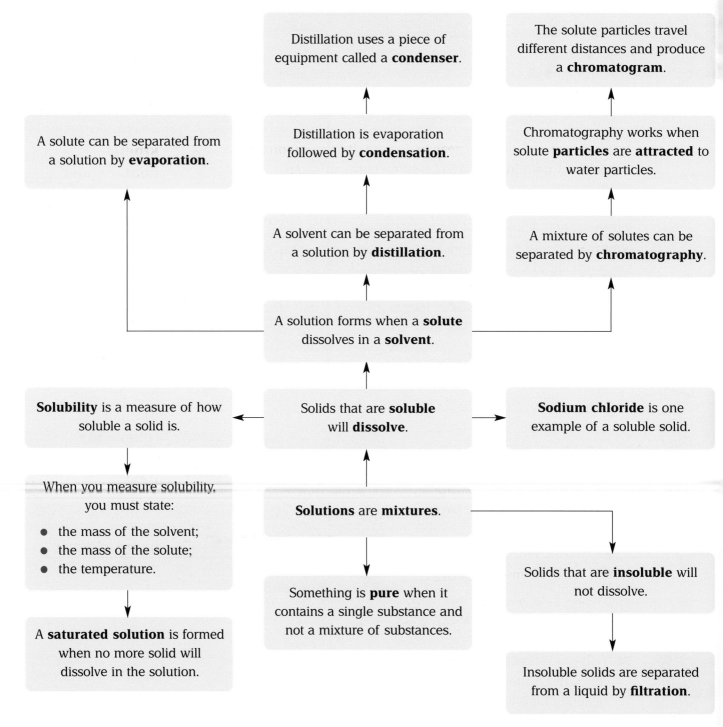

Distillation uses a piece of equipment called a **condenser**.

The solute particles travel different distances and produce a **chromatogram**.

A solute can be separated from a solution by **evaporation**.

Distillation is evaporation followed by **condensation**.

Chromatography works when solute **particles** are **attracted** to water particles.

A solvent can be separated from a solution by **distillation**.

A mixture of solutes can be separated by **chromatography**.

A solution forms when a **solute** dissolves in a **solvent**.

Solubility is a measure of how soluble a solid is.

Solids that are **soluble** will **dissolve**.

Sodium chloride is one example of a soluble solid.

When you measure solubility, you must state:

- the mass of the solvent;
- the mass of the solute;
- the temperature.

Solutions are **mixtures**.

A **saturated solution** is formed when no more solid will dissolve in the solution.

Something is **pure** when it contains a single substance and not a mixture of substances.

Solids that are **insoluble** will not dissolve.

Insoluble solids are separated from a liquid by **filtration**.

Energy resources

In this unit we shall be studying what energy is and how we use it.

71.1 Energy and fuels

Energy is one of the big ideas in science. It is so important that it has its own unit, **joules**. We measure energy in joules.

What energy is

Anything that involves energy change can be called work. Nothing can happen without energy making it happen.

The microwave oven needs energy to cook.

The cheetah needs energy to run.

The rocket needs energy to take off.

The plant needs energy to grow.

To do work energy must change in some way. It can:

● move from one place to another – this is called energy <u>transfer</u>;

● change from one type of energy to another – this is called <u>transformation</u>.

1   What is meant by energy?

2   What must energy do to make things happen?

3   Make a list of <u>six</u> things that you think need energy to make them happen or work.

KEY WORDS
energy
joules
gravitational potential
chemical
kinetic
heat
light
elastic potential
electrical
sound
engine
Bunsen burner
fossil fuel
coal
mineral oil
natural gas
non-renewable
renewable
wind
tidal
solar
wave
hydro-electric
geothermal
biomass

There are different types of energy

We are surrounded by different types of energy. Once you know what they are, you can spot them everywhere.

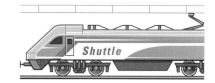

Gravitational potential energy is stored in things which are high up.

Fuels store **chemical energy**.

A moving object has **kinetic energy**.

Heat energy is given out by hot objects.

Light energy is given out by luminous objects.

Elastic potential energy is stored in things which are squashed or stretched.

Electrical energy is the energy carried by electricity.

Sound energy is given out by loudspeakers.

4   Name the eight types of energy.

5   List any types of energy that are present in your classroom.

Making things happen

We know that energy needs to change from one type to another to make things happen. We can show some of these changes using an energy transformation diagram. The picture shows an example:

6   What type of energy does a kettle transform electrical energy into?

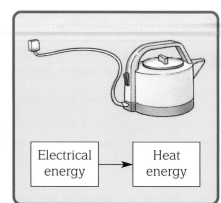

| Electrical energy | → | Heat energy |

7   What useful energy does a bulb transform electrical energy into?

Useful fuels

Fuels have chemical energy stored in them. We burn fuels to release this stored energy as heat. We use the energy to make lots of useful things happen.

- Most of our electrical energy comes from burning fuels in power stations. This is then transformed into electrical energy by generators.

- In the science laboratory you will use a Bunsen burner. This burns methane or propane gas to release heat energy.

In everyday life we use lots of different fuels to do different jobs. In a car this fuel is usually petrol or diesel. It burns inside the **engine**.

8 Look at the five pictures showing different fuels being used. Then, list <u>five</u> common fuels.

9 What fuel can be used instead of petrol and diesel?

10 Which fuel was used to light street lights in the 19th century?

We burn fuels to do jobs for us. These jobs mainly fall into one of four categories: transport, heating, cooking and making electricity.

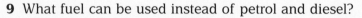
Oil is used to heat schools.

Aircraft use aviation fuel.

Gas is used to cook.

Coal is used to generate electricity.

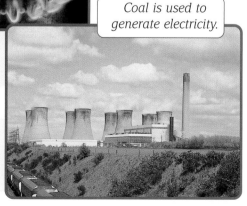

11 What are the <u>four</u> main categories of uses for fuels?

12 Which fuels can be used to heat our homes ?

13 Name a fuel (other than the one shown in the picture) that can be used in a power station.

Using a Bunsen burner safely

The **Bunsen burner** was invented in 1855 by a German chemist called Robert Bunsen. It burns methane or propane to produce a hot flame. To use it safely, you must follow these important safety rules:

Step 1: Safety goggles (eye protection) must be worn all the time.

Step 2: Long hair must be tied back. All loose clothing must be tucked in.

Step 3: The Bunsen burner should be placed on the middle of a heatproof mat, in the middle of your bench. Securely attach the side tube to the gas tap.

Step 4: Light the Bunsen burner with the air hole closed, at arm's length using a lighted splint. Do not turn on the gas until the lighted splint is above the barrel of the Bunsen burner.

It is important that you follow the other important lab rules as well, such as never running in a lab.

The size of the flame is controlled using the gas tap. The type of flame is controlled by opening and closing the air hole.

14 Who invented the Bunsen burner?

15 How do you control the type of flame?

16 The unit for energy is the joule. Try and find out as much as you can about James Joule. Try making a time-line of his life or write a short biography.

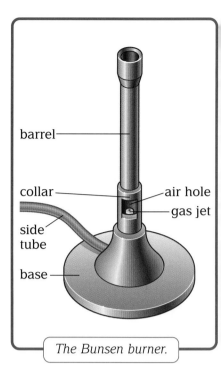

The Bunsen burner.

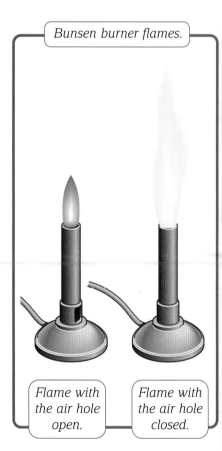

Bunsen burner flames.

Flame with the air hole open.

Flame with the air hole closed.

71.2 Fossil fuels

Fossil fuels, like **coal**, **mineral oil** and **natural gas** come from plants and animals that died millions of years ago. They are very important to us as fuels and for making materials like plastics.

Fossil fuels are made from dead plants and animals

Fossil fuels were made millions of years ago from the remains of dead plants and animals. You can see the fossilised remains of plants in coal.

The piece of coal has the fossilised remains of a plant in it.

How coal was formed.

Trees store energy from sunlight as they grow.

Dead trees fall into swamps.

The dead trees are buried under layers of mud.

The wood gradually turns into coal.

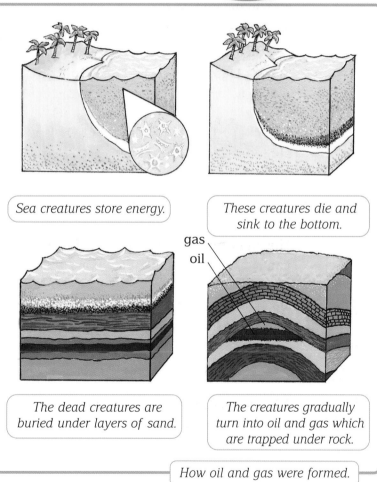

Sea creatures store energy.

These creatures die and sink to the bottom.

gas

oil

The dead creatures are buried under layers of sand.

The creatures gradually turn into oil and gas which are trapped under rock.

How oil and gas were formed.

1   Where does the chemical energy in fossil fuels come from?

2   How do oil and gas become trapped? How do we get at them?

Fossil fuels will run out

All the fossil fuels take many millions of years to form. We are using them up far faster than they are being replaced. Fossil fuels are **non-renewable**. This means that one day they will run out. It is estimated that we have enough coal to last 300 years, enough gas to last 60 years and enough oil to last 40 years. These estimates assume that we will keep using them at the same rate we do today and that no more fossil fuels will be discovered.

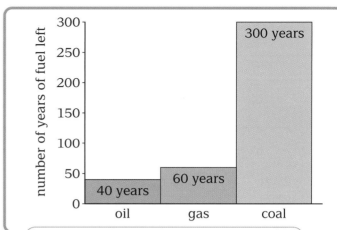

Bar chart showing when fossil fuels will run out based on current rates of consumption of known world reserves.

3 Fossil fuels are <u>non-renewable</u>. What does this mean?

4 How old will you be when oil runs out, if oil runs out in the time shown in the bar chart?

5 How long do you think fossil fuels will actually last ? State your reasons.

How we use fossil fuels is always changing

The Industrial Revolution happened in Britain before anywhere else. People started to work in large factories and use lots of machines. The fuel they used was coal. Britain had plenty of coal, underground. Men, women and children worked in dark, dirty and dangerous coal mines, to get it. The picture shows this.

Today, in Britain, coal has become less popular. Natural gas, which comes from the North Sea, is being used more and more, because it burns more cleanly.

Mineral oil has become increasingly popular, since it was first drilled for in Pennsylvania, USA, in 1859. This is because of the ever increasing numbers of cars and other vehicles across the world. In the future, fossil fuel use is likely to increase as more and more countries become industrialised.

6 Why is coal being used less and less in Britain today?

7 Why is the use of fossil fuels likely to increase across the world, despite the pollution it causes?

We use fossil fuels to make most of our electricity

We need electricity for every part of our lives, at home and at work. Most of our electrical energy is transformed from the chemical energy in fuels. The table shows advantages and disadvantages of different fossil fuels used to make electricity.

Fossil fuels	Advantages	Disadvantages
Coal, mineral oil and natural gas	Reliable, concentrated forms of energy	Need to be transported and stored; burning them contributes to global warming
Coal	Plentiful supply	Burning it contributes to acid rain
Mineral oil	Can transport it in pipes	Bad sea pollution possible from oil spills from tankers
Natural gas	Burns more cleanly than others	Difficult to drill for

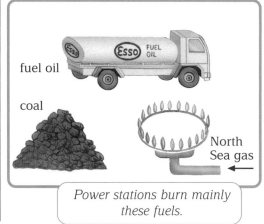

fuel oil

coal

North Sea gas

Power stations burn mainly these fuels.

8 Where does most of our electrical energy come from?

9 What is an advantage of using natural gas to produce electricity?

10 What is a disadvantage of using coal to produce electricity?

It is important to save fuels

It is important to save fossil fuels because they are running out and because burning them is the main cause of air pollution. This air pollution is causing problems such as global warming, acid rain and smog. Fuels can be saved by expanding the use of renewable energy resources, which you will find out about next, and by using machines that need less energy to do the same job, such as energy efficient light bulbs.

11 What are the <u>two</u> reasons why it is important to save fuels?

Gases from car exhausts cause air pollution.

12 Why does the cyclist in the picture need to wear an air filter?

Lots of countries also generate electricity in nuclear power stations. These generate a lot of heat energy that then gets converted into electricity. Nuclear reactors give out dangerous radiation. So thick walls are built around them to protect us.

13 Find out what happened at the Chernobyl nuclear power station in 1986. It has made a lot of people worry about nuclear power stations.

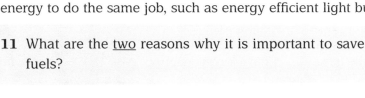

71.3 Renewable energy resources

Fossil fuels will run out one day. We say they are non-renewable. They also cause pollution. This has led to the development of alternatives to fossil fuels. Many of these alternatives are **renewable** energy resources. They will never run out.

Renewable energy resources won't run out

In the future, renewable energy resources will play a bigger role. Renewable energy resources, such as **wind** energy and **tidal** energy, will last almost for ever. As we use them, they are naturally topped up by a fresh supply.

1   How long will renewable energy resources last?

2   Name a renewable energy resource.

The Sun will keep on shining for about 5 billion more years.

So **solar** energy is a renewable energy resource.

Most renewable energy resources depend on the Sun

The diagrams show how the **wind**, a **wave** on the sea and hydro-electric power stations get their energy from the Sun.

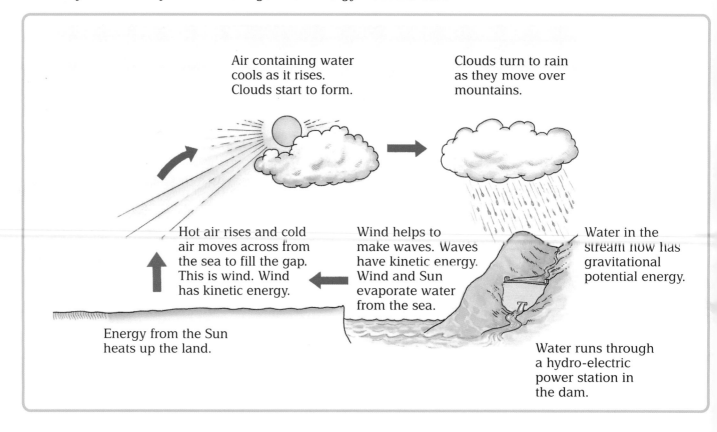

Air containing water cools as it rises. Clouds start to form.

Clouds turn to rain as they move over mountains.

Hot air rises and cold air moves across from the sea to fill the gap. This is wind. Wind has kinetic energy.

Wind helps to make waves. Waves have kinetic energy. Wind and Sun evaporate water from the sea.

Water in the stream now has gravitational potential energy.

Energy from the Sun heats up the land.

Water runs through a hydro-electric power station in the dam.

Not all renewable energy resources depend on the Sun. Tidal energy comes from the gravitational pull of the Moon (and the Sun). **Geothermal** energy comes from the heat energy in hot rocks deep underground.

3 Name <u>two</u> renewable energy resources that depend on the Sun.

4 Name <u>two</u> renewable energy resources that don't depend on the Sun.

5 Explain how energy from the Sun makes the wind blow.

6 Explain why hydro-electric energy comes from the Sun.

Trees need energy from the Sun to grow. This energy is stored in all the material from which the plant is made, including the wood. It is known as **biomass** energy.

7 Explain what biomass energy is.

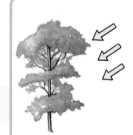

Energy is transferred to trees by sunlight. Trees store this energy as they grow. So trees are stores of chemical energy. You can burn the wood as a fuel.

8 How can that energy be released from wood?

9 Look at the table on pages 114–115. What is a disadvantage of tidal energy?

10 What is an advantage of all renewable energy resources?

11 Wood could be described as both renewable and non-renewable. Explain why.

There are lots of renewable energy resources

It is difficult to work out how expensive renewable energy resources really are. Read the table to find out about them.

Name of renewable energy resource	Solar energy	Wind energy	Tidal energy
Ultimate source of energy	The Sun	The Sun	Moon's gravitational pull
How it is used	Solar cells turn the Sun's energy directly into electricity. Solar panels on roofs convert solar energy into heat energy.	The kinetic energy of the wind is used to turn large turbines, which drive generators which convert the kinetic energy into electricity.	A barrier called a barrage is built across the estuary (tidal mouth of a river). This acts as a dam. As water is brought in by the tides it gets trapped in the estuary. As this trapped water returns to the sea, it drives turbines in the barrage,which in turn drive generators.
An advantage	Solar cells are useful for portable devices like radios.	Technology well developed	No pollution
A disadvantage	Still quite expensive	Wind turbines look ugly	Building cost is very large.
	solar energy array of solar cells solar energy solar panel	wind → turbine generator The wind makes the turbine turn. This drives the generator.	When the barrage is built the mud flats in the estuary are flooded all the time.

Hydro-electricity	Biomass energy	Wave energy	Geothermal energy
Gravitational potential energy	The Sun	The Sun	Heat energy in hot rocks deep underground
Water trapped behind a dam is used to make electricity, by letting water flow downhill.	Biomass is the energy stored in plant material like wood. There are lots of ways of releasing this energy. For example, sugar from sugar cane can be converted into alcohol, which can then be used as a fuel for cars.	The up-and-down movement of sea water can be used to make electricity.	Cold water is pumped deep underground, in a suitable place. It comes back up as steam. The energy in the steam is used to make electricity.
No pollution	Using biomass energy more means using fossil fuels less.	No pollution	Low levels of general pollution.
Areas of land may be flooded.	Burning releases carbon dioxide.	Corrosion of machinery by the salty water	Sulphurous smell can be a problem locally.
		Water moves up and down inside the tube. This drives air through the turbine.	

71.4 Living things and energy

All living things, including us, use energy. All activity, including just being alive, needs energy. Food is the energy resource that animals and plants need to live and do things.

We need energy from food for everything we do

Different activities need different amounts of energy. If you lift an apple up 1 m, it uses 1 J of energy. A joule isn't much energy at all, so sometimes the kilojoule is used. 1 kilojoule is the same as 1000 joules. The pictures show how much energy different activities use every minute.

Jogging needs 60 kilojoules of energy for every minute you jog.

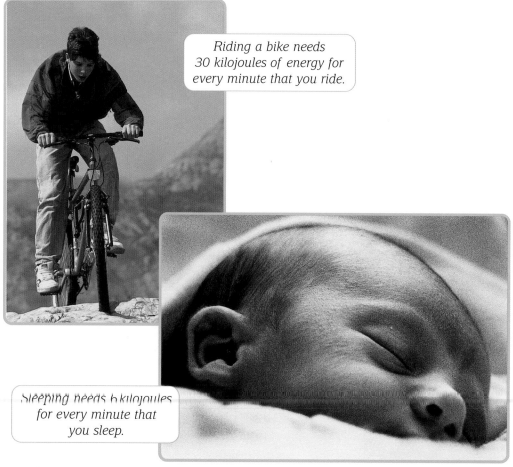

Riding a bike needs 30 kilojoules of energy for every minute that you ride.

Sleeping needs 6 kilojoules for every minute that you sleep.

Walking needs 20 kilojoules for every minute you are strolling along.

1 Which of the four activities needs the least energy?

2 Can you think of any other things that might affect the amount of energy a person needs?

Animals eat food to get their energy

Animals need to eat food to get energy. If you look on food labels you can see that there is an old unit for energy used as well. This is called the kilocalorie (kcal). This is just like having two different units for length: centimetres and inches. Either unit tells you how much chemical energy is stored in food.

Nutrition labels

Food a

NUTRITION INFORMATION
100 g provides: Energy 1500 kJ / 370 kcal. Protein 4.5 g. Carbohydrate 67 g. (of which sugars 29 g) (starch 33 g). Fat 10 g (of which saturates 2 g). Fibre 3 g. Sodium 0.3 g. Vitamins: Thiamin B_1 1 mg (70%). Riboflavin B_2 1.1 mg (70%). Niacin 12 mg (70%). Vitamin B_6 1.4 mg (70%). Folic Acid 135 µg (70%). Vitamin B_{12} 0.7 µg (70%). Minerals: Calcium 540 mg (70%). Iron 6.4 mg (45%).

Food b

NUTRITION INFORMATION	PER PIECE	PER 100 g
ENERGY:	1180 kJ / 281 kcal	1885 kJ / 449 kcal
PROTEIN:	2.6 g	4.2 g
CARBOHYDRATE:	43.1 g	69.0 g
FAT:	10.9 g	17.4 g

3 Which of the two foods has more energy per 100 g?

4 What type of energy is stored in food?

The physicist John Tyndall worked out that the energy he needed to climb a mountain called the Matterhorn was contained in a ham sandwich, so that was all the food he took with him!

The potato plant uses the energy in sunlight to make its food.

The energy in food comes from the Sun

Like all living things, plants need food to live and grow. Unlike animals, they make their own food using the energy in sunlight. Patrick eats meat, which comes from an animal. The animal he eats got its energy in the first place from plants. The plants got their energy to live and grow from the Sun. So, all our food energy resources originally came from the Sun.

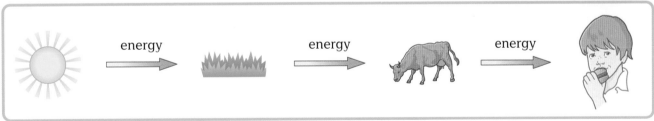

5 Where do plants get the energy from to make their food?

6 How are animals and plants different, in terms of the food they need?

7 Why is it more energy efficient to eat plants rather than animals?

You should now know the meaning of these words:

fossil fuel	mineral oil	hydro-electric	heat
Bunsen burner	natural gas	solar	sound
renewable	biomass	wave	light
non-renewable	wind	chemical	gravitational potential
joules	geothermal	kinetic	elastic potential
coal	tidal	electrical	engine

You should also have an understanding of these key ideas:

- **Energy** is the ability to do work. It is measured in **joules**.

- There are different types of energy such as **kinetic** energy and **heat** energy.

- Fuels are very important in our lives. We have many different fuels that we use.

- The energy that fuels release is useful for transport, heating, cooking and making electricity.

- The **Bunsen burner** is used in the school laboratory to release energy for doing experiments. It is important to follow the safety rules when using it.

- **Fossil fuels** are made from dead plants and animals. They formed over millions of years.

- Fossil fuels will run out. They are **non-renewable**.

- We use fossil fuels to make most of our electricity.

- It is important to save fuels because they are running out and because burning them causes air pollution.

- **Renewable** energy resources such as **wind** energy won't run out as long as the Sun keeps shining.

- Most renewable energy resources depend on the Sun.

- There are lots of renewable energy resources, such as **geothermal** energy and **solar** energy.

- Renewable energy resources do not cause air pollution.

- Animals eat food to get their energy. The energy in food is measured in kilojoules or kilocalories.

- Activities that we do all need energy. We get the energy we need from the chemical energy in food.

- Plants make food using the energy in sunlight.

- All the energy in food ultimately comes from the Sun.

- We need to balance the energy in our diet.

Electrical circuits

In this unit we shall be finding out how electrical circuits work and how electricity can be used safely in the home.

7J.1 How electrical circuits work

We use electrical devices in our everyday lives, but we often don't think about how they are put together. We are going to study how to connect electrical components together to make a **circuit** which works.

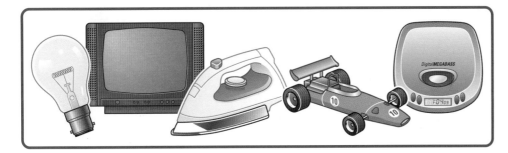

Making a circuit

Electricity will only flow when a circuit is complete. These diagrams show four attempts at making a **bulb** light up. Only one will work.

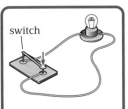

switch

There is no source of energy to make the electricity flow, so the bulb will not light up.

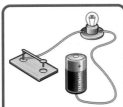

There is a gap. It is not a complete circuit, so the electricity cannot flow around.

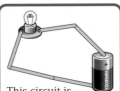

This circuit is connected using wood. Wood does not let electricity flow through it. Wood is not a conductor.

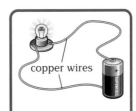

copper wires

This is a complete circuit, electricity can flow and the bulb will light up.

1   Describe how you would need to connect a battery, bulb and switch so that the bulb lights up. Draw a picture of this.

2   What sort of material would you need to use to make leads to connect an electrical circuit?

Using a switch

Sometimes we need to be able to break the circuit to stop the electricity flowing. We can do this by using a **switch**. When a switch is <u>closed</u> the circuit is complete and electricity can flow. When the switch is <u>open</u> the circuit is not complete so electricity cannot flow. We often say that we 'switch something on'. This means that a switch is closed to make a circuit.

A torch is a device that contains a simple circuit. A battery is connected to a switch and a bulb. When the torch is needed the switch can be closed so that the bulb lights up. When the torch is not needed, the switch can be opened to prevent the battery running down.

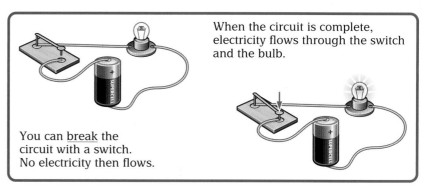

When the circuit is complete, electricity flows through the switch and the bulb.

You can <u>break</u> the circuit with a switch. No electricity then flows.

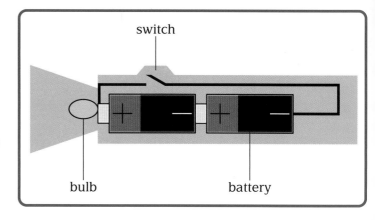

switch

bulb   battery

3 How does a switch turn off the bulb in a torch?

4 When we 'switch an appliance on' what change are we making to the circuit?

5 Why do you need a switch in a torch?

Drawing a circuit

It is useful to have a quick way of drawing the components in a circuit. Instead of drawing pictures we can draw symbols to represent the components. It is important to remember these symbols and use them when drawing your circuits.

You will find out about other symbols later in the unit.

Component	Symbol
Cell	
Battery	
Connection	
Open switch	
Closed switch	
Bulb	

We can now use these symbols to draw circuit diagrams.
This is the circuit diagram for the torch.

Look carefully at these four circuit pictures and use them to answer questions 6 and 7.

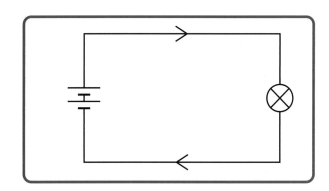

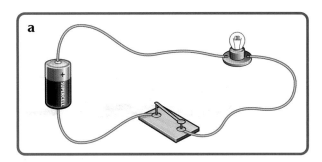

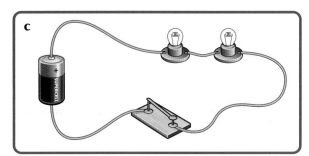

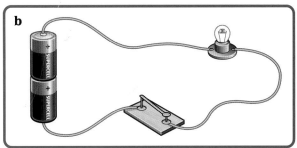

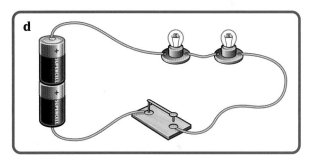

6 Draw circuit diagrams for each of the four circuits.

7 **a** In which of these circuits will the bulb not light up?

b In which of these circuits <u>do you think</u> the bulb or bulbs will be brightest?

8 In some houses the light on the landing can be switched on upstairs or downstairs. Either design or research a circuit which could use two switches to operate one bulb. The bulb must light up when you close one switch or the other, not both.

7J.2 Inside a circuit

We are now going to look at what is happening inside a circuit once it is connected up. We are also going to find out how to change the brightness of a bulb in a circuit.

Series circuits

In a **series** circuit all components are connected in one loop. This diagram shows a circuit with two bulbs in series.

In this circuit there is only one path around the circuit for the electricity to follow, so all the electricity flows through all the components in the circuit. Bulbs are not the only components that can be connected in series. You need to choose the components for the job you want the circuit to perform.

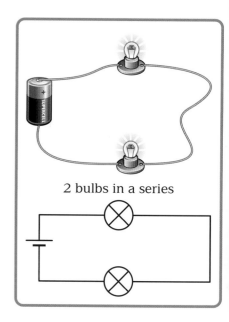

2 bulbs in a series

1 What is a series circuit?

2 What power supply is used in the circuit above?

Electric current

In a complete circuit we say that there is an electric **current** which flows around the circuit. We say that this current flows from the positive side of the **power supply**, around the circuit and back to the negative side of the power supply.

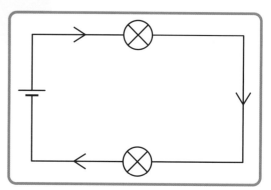

3 Which way does the electric current flow around a circuit?

We can measure the electric current in any circuit by using an **ammeter**. An ammeter tells us the value of the current in amperes (**amps** or 'A' for short). This picture shows an ammeter showing a reading of 0.15 A.

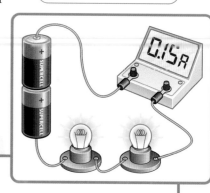

This is the symbol for an ammeter.

When we use an ammeter in a circuit we connect it in series with the other components. This means that all of the current flows through the ammeter. The diagram shows how the ammeter should be connected.

4 What unit do we use to measure the electric current?

5 Describe how an ammeter should be connected in a circuit.

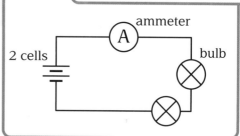

Measuring electric current in a series circuit

These three diagrams show the positions in which an ammeter could be connected in this series circuit.

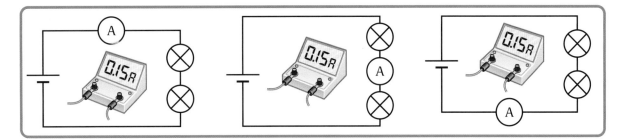

All of these ammeters show the same reading. The electric current is the same all the way around a series circuit. The current does not get used up as it passes through each bulb; it stays the same.

6 What would be the readings on ammeters X and Y in this circuit?

7 How does the current in front of a bulb compare to the current after the bulb?

Changing the current

Dimmer switches can be used with household lights to change the brightness of the bulb. The circuits show three different dimmer switch settings and how these affect the brightness of the bulbs.

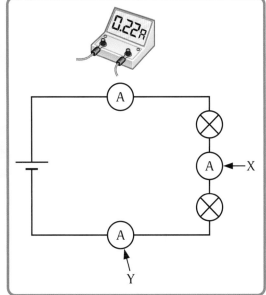

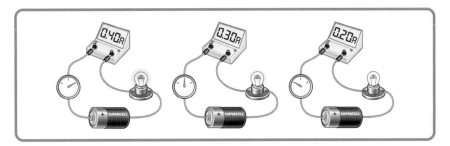

When a current flows in a circuit it has to push its way through each component. It is held back very slightly by each new component it has to push through. This causes **resistance** in a circuit.

As the dimmer switch is turned the bulbs get less bright and the current decreases. A dimmer switch is an example of a **variable resistor**. As you turn the dimmer switch you change the resistance. Increasing the resistance decreases the current and makes the bulb dimmer. Decreasing the resistance increases the current and makes the bulb brighter.

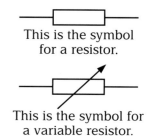

This is the symbol for a resistor.

This is the symbol for a variable resistor.

8 What does a dimmer switch change in a circuit?

9 In a house, when a dimmer switch is turned a bulb gets brighter.

    a Is the resistance increasing or decreasing?

    b Is the current increasing or decreasing?

More bulbs

Bulbs have resistance. They 'resist' or 'slow down' the flow of electric current. Changing the number of bulbs in a series circuit changes the resistance of that circuit. A bulb is one example of a **resistor**. All components cause resistance just like bulbs do.

As bulbs are added to this circuit the total resistance increases and the current decreases. As the current decreases, the bulbs become less bright.

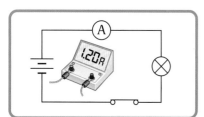 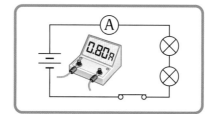 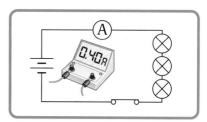

10 Does the total resistance increase or decrease as you add bulbs in a series circuit?

11 When you increase the number of bulbs in a series circuit, what happens to the brightness of those bulbs?

12 Resistors are used in many devices to change the current in that device. Research different uses for resistors and explain what effect the resistor has in each circuit.

7J.3 Energy for the circuit

For an electric current to flow around a circuit there needs to be a source of energy. A cell or battery provides this energy to 'push' the current around the circuit.

Cells and batteries

This picture shows a torch. The energy to make this torch light up is supplied by two **cells**. Two or more cells connected together are called a **battery**.

switch

bulb   battery

Cells and batteries are marked to show their **voltage**. The voltage is measured in **volts**, or 'V' for short.

A higher voltage means that more energy can be supplied. So higher voltage means brighter bulbs.

Be careful! If the voltage is too high the bulb will 'blow' and stop working.

A 1.5V cell.

Two 1.5V cells make a 3.0V battery.

Three 1.5V cells make a 4.5V battery.

A 9V cell.

1 What is the difference between a cell and a battery?

2 If you connected four 1.5 V cells together, what would be the total voltage?

3 You increase the voltage supplied to a circuit.

   a What would happen to the brightness of the bulbs?

   b Using your answer to part **a**, explain what will happen to the current if the voltage is increased.

Inside a cell

When a cell is connected in a circuit, it pushes the current around the circuit. Inside the cell are chemicals which react together. It is this chemical reaction which pushes the current.

When you connect cells together to make a battery, you need to make sure that the positive end of one cell is connected to the negative end of the next.

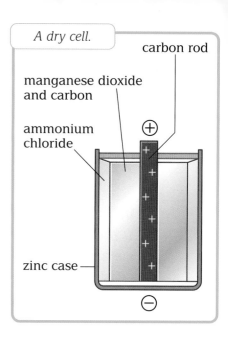

A dry cell.

carbon rod

manganese dioxide and carbon

ammonium chloride

⊕

zinc case

⊖

4 What chemicals can be found inside a dry cell?

5 Draw a picture of a battery of three cells connected correctly.

Inside a circuit

It can be difficult to picture what happens in an electric circuit because you can't see anything moving. The flow of electric current around a circuit can be compared to the flow of water around a system of pipes.

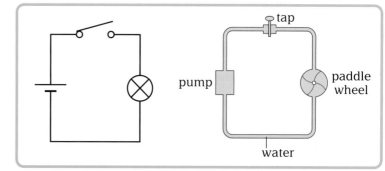

tap

pump

paddle wheel

water

6 a What flows around an electric circuit?

   b What makes this flow?

7 a What would happen to the flow of water if you used two pumps?

   b What would be the equivalent in an electric circuit?

Electric circuit		Water circuit	
OBJECT	**JOB**	**OBJECT**	**JOB**
Battery	Pushes the current around the circuit	Pump	Pushes the water around the circuit
Current	Flows around the circuit	Water	Flows around the circuit
Bulb	Uses energy from the current and holds back the current	Paddle wheel	Uses energy from the water and slows the water down
Switch	Breaks the circuit and the flow of current	Tap	Stops the flow of water

8 Some types of cell can be recharged. Find out about the different types of rechargeable cell. Include in your research which chemicals are used in each type of cell. You can also find out how much charge the cell can hold (usually measured in AmpHours).

7J.4 Parallel circuits

So far, the circuits we have studied have been series circuits. The other main type of circuit is called a **parallel** circuit. We will now find out more about parallel circuits and their uses.

Bulbs in parallel

In the series circuits that we have studied so far, there is just one route for the current around the circuit. In parallel circuits there are always junctions where the current can go along two or more different routes.

This circuit shows two bulbs connected in parallel. The electric current leaves the battery. When it gets to junction A some of the current goes through bulb 1 and some through bulb 2. The current splits up. When the current reaches junction B it joins back together again and travels back to the battery. Each part of the circuit, through bulb A and bulb B, is called a 'branch' of the circuit.

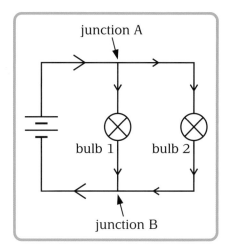

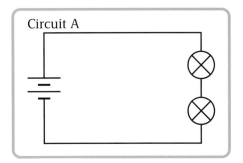
Circuit A

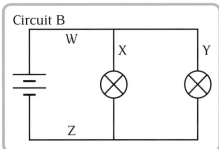
Circuit B

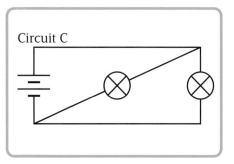
Circuit C

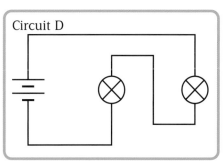
Circuit D

1 Look at the four circuits, A to D.

   a Which circuits are series circuits?

   b Which circuits are parallel circuits?

2 How many routes can the electric current go in:

   a a series circuit?   **b** a parallel circuit?

3 In circuit B the current is at its highest value in the position marked W. Where else would the current be at its highest value: at X, Y or Z?

Electric current in parallel circuits

In a parallel circuit the total current from the battery is the same as the current through each of the separate branches added together. This diagram shows two identical bulbs connected in parallel; these bulbs have the same resistance. The electric current flowing through each bulb is the same, 0.5 A. The current from the battery is the same as the current through the bulbs added together:

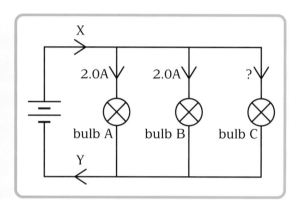

$$0.5\,A + 0.5\,A = 1.0\,A$$

4 In this circuit the three bulbs are identical. Use this circuit diagram to answer the following questions.

a What is the current through bulb C?

b What is the current from the battery?

c What is the current in position X?

d What is the current in position Y?

Bright bulbs in parallel

In a parallel circuit each bulb is connected directly to the battery. The voltage across each bulb is the same as the voltage across the battery. This means that all of the bulbs are bright. You can connect as many bulbs as you like in parallel and they will always stay the same brightness.

When you connect more bulbs in parallel, the current from the battery increases. If you have a lot of bulbs connected the battery will go flat very quickly.

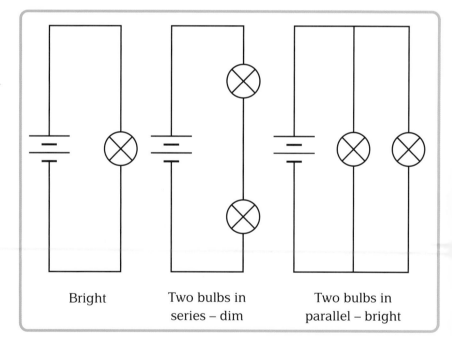

5 If you have four bulbs connected in parallel with a 3 V battery, what will be the voltage across each of the bulbs?

6 As you add lots of bulbs in parallel, what happens to:

a the brightness **b** the total resistance

c the total current through the bulbs **d** the battery

Series or parallel

When designing an electrical circuit you need to consider whether a series or a parallel circuit is the best for the intended use. Some Christmas tree lights are wired in series, whereas the lights in houses are wired in parallel.

The parallel circuit is better if you want to control the bulbs separately. This is what you want for the lights in a house. The series circuit can be safer because the current is smaller. A series circuit is useful if you want to light several bulbs which do not need to be very bright.

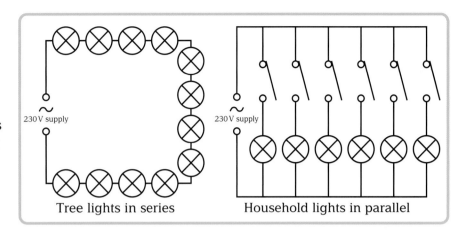

230 V supply

Tree lights in series

230 V supply

Household lights in parallel

Series circuit	Parallel circuit
If one bulb blows they all go out.	If one bulb blows only that one goes out.
One switch operates all of the bulbs.	Each bulb can be turned on and off with its own switch.
The voltage across the power supply is shared between all of the bulbs.	The voltage across each bulb is the same as across the power supply.
The current from the power supply is low.	The current from the power supply is high.

7 What happens to the other bulbs in a series circuit if one bulb blows?

8 Ten bulbs were connected in a series circuit to a power supply. Ten identical bulbs were connected in a parallel circuit to an identical power supply.

   a Which circuit would have the highest voltage across each bulb?

   b In which circuit would the bulbs be brighter?

   c Which circuit do you think would use the most electricity?

9 A Christmas tree light manufacturer wants to design tree lights with 12 bulbs: 3 red, 3 blue, 3 green and 3 yellow. He wants to be able to turn all three bulbs of the same colour on and off together. If a bulb of one colour blows, all of the bulbs of that colour could be off but the other colours should still be capable of being switched on. Design a circuit for this manufacturer.

Electricity is very useful but also potentially very dangerous. We need to protect ourselves when using electricity, especially when it is **mains electricity**, which uses a higher voltage than batteries.

Safety at home

Most accidents when using electricity in the home are caused by carelessness. If you follow a few sensible safety precautions you will reduce the danger. Here are some reminders of things you must never do.

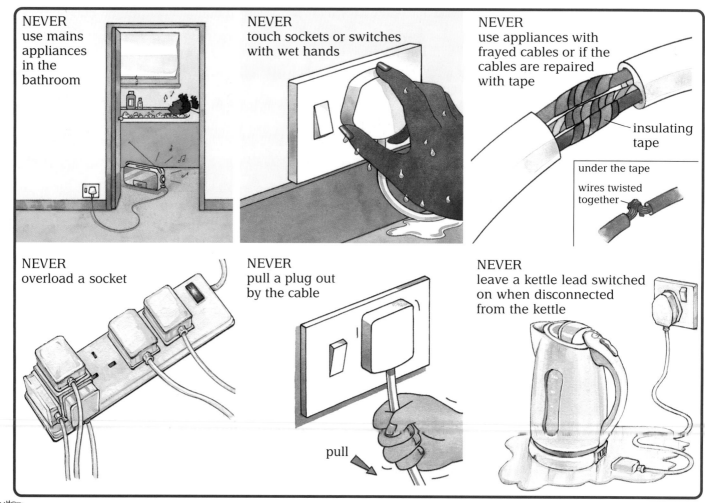

NEVER use mains appliances in the bathroom

NEVER touch sockets or switches with wet hands

NEVER use appliances with frayed cables or if the cables are repaired with tape

insulating tape

under the tape
wires twisted together

NEVER overload a socket

NEVER pull a plug out by the cable

NEVER leave a kettle lead switched on when disconnected from the kettle

pull

1 List <u>six</u> things you should never do when using mains electricity.

2 How should you pull a plug out of a socket?

3 What could you use as a safe alternative to a mains powered radio in the bathroom?

Fuses

Sometimes a fault in a circuit can cause the electric current to become too big. This can damage electrical appliances. A **fuse** breaks the circuit if the current becomes too big. This stops the appliance from working and therefore protects it. This is the circuit symbol for a fuse:

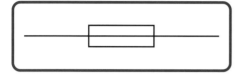

Inside a fuse is a piece of wire, called fuse wire. If the current is too high the fuse wire becomes hot and melts. When the fuse wire melts the circuit is broken and no current can now flow. The word 'fuse' is another word for melt.

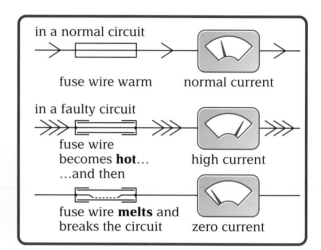

in a normal circuit

fuse wire warm   normal current

in a faulty circuit

fuse wire becomes **hot**…   high current
…and then

fuse wire **melts** and breaks the circuit   zero current

4 **a** What happens to the wire inside a fuse if the current is too high?

b How does this stop the flow of electric current?

You can find fuses in plugs. The fuse is always connected to the live wire so that no electric current can flow to the appliance if the fuse blows. Fuses have different current ratings; this is the current above which the fuse will blow. The fuse drawn here has a current rating of 5 A. If a current of more than 5 A flows the fuse will blow.

Circuit breakers are often used instead of fuses. These 'cut out' when the current is too high and can be reset by flicking a switch.

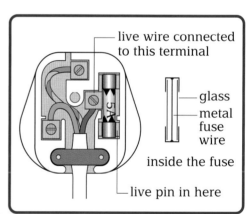

live wire connected to this terminal

glass

metal fuse wire

inside the fuse

live pin in here

5 A fuse in a plug could be replaced with an iron nail and the appliance would still work. Why must you not do this?

6 Try to find out what values of current rating fuses you can get. For each value list as many appliances as you can which should take this size of fuse.

7J.6 Discovering electricity

So far in this unit we have used the idea of electric current and the fact that it flows through circuits. We are now going to consider where the idea of electric current came from and find out a little about the scientists who discovered it.

Luigi Galvani and his frogs

Luigi Galvani was an Italian scientist born in 1737. His main interest was in medicine and how the body works. He worked at the University of Bologna. This is where he started a series of experiments in 1780. As part of his experimental work he was studying the legs of frogs. These frog legs were hung up by copper hooks, on iron railings. Galvani noticed that the frog legs twitched and the muscles contracted.

Scientists believed that **nerves** carried messages around the body. Most scientists thought that these nerves were pipes carrying water. Galvani now believed that these nerves carried electrical pulses. This electricity must be generated somewhere inside the body.

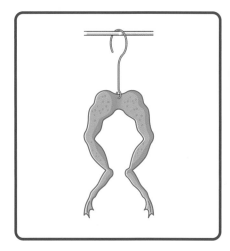

1   What is the job of these nerves?
2   What do nerves carry to the muscles?

Alessandro Volta and his cell

Alessandro Volta was another Italian scientist. He was born in 1745. Volta realised that there must be some sort of reaction between the copper hooks, the iron railings and the liquids from inside the frog. It was this reaction which produced the electric current which travelled along the nerves in the frog's legs.

Volta used this information to make the first ever electric cell. He made this cell using discs made of the metals silver and zinc separated by cardboard discs soaked in salt solution. The volt is named after Volta in honour of the fact that he made the first ever electric cell.

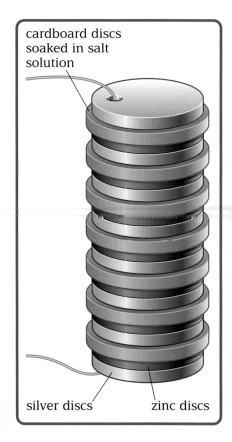

cardboard discs soaked in salt solution

silver discs   zinc discs

3   What did Volta use to make the first electric cell?
4   Which unit is named after Volta?

5   Galvani deduced that electric currents travelled along nerves. Volta made the first battery. How could Volta's battery be used to prove that nerves carry an electric current?

You should now understand the key words and key ideas shown below.

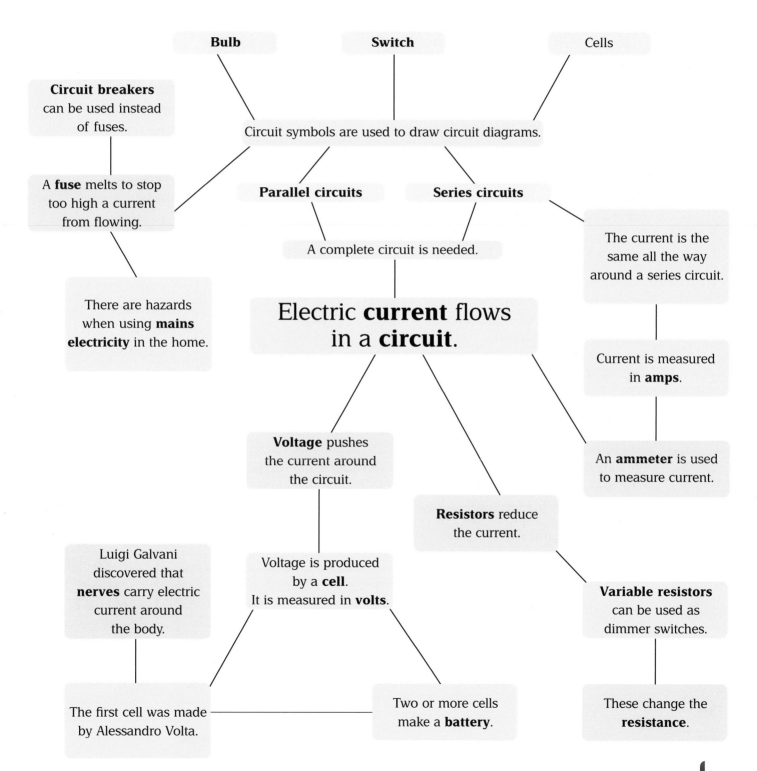

Bulb

Switch

Cells

Circuit breakers can be used instead of fuses.

Circuit symbols are used to draw circuit diagrams.

A **fuse** melts to stop too high a current from flowing.

Parallel circuits

Series circuits

The current is the same all the way around a series circuit.

A complete circuit is needed.

There are hazards when using **mains electricity** in the home.

Electric **current** flows in a **circuit**.

Current is measured in **amps**.

Voltage pushes the current around the circuit.

An **ammeter** is used to measure current.

Resistors reduce the current.

Luigi Galvani discovered that **nerves** carry electric current around the body.

Voltage is produced by a **cell**. It is measured in **volts**.

Variable resistors can be used as dimmer switches.

The first cell was made by Alessandro Volta.

Two or more cells make a **battery**.

These change the **resistance**.

7K

Forces and their effects

In this unit we shall study the effect that different forces have on objects. We shall learn the names of some forces and study ideas connected with the speed of objects.

KEY WORDS
force
newton
stretch
attraction
repulsion
weight
body
gravity
mass
extension
proportional
upthrust
density
volume
friction
lubricant
drag
speed
distance

7K.1 Where we come across forces

In everyday life there are many different examples of **force**. They are all pushes or pulls.

Forces act in pairs

When things touch there are two forces acting in opposite directions, one force on each object. When the legs of a stool touch the floor there are push forces on the legs and push forces on the floor.

When you carry a bag, the handles and your hand touch each other. Two forces are produced where your hand and the bag touch. There is a pull force downwards from the bag on your hand and a pull force upwards from your hand on the bag. You can show these forces on a diagram with arrows. The length of the arrow shows how big the force is.

Look at the pictures of the person and the book.

1 Does the up or down arrow show the force of the person on the floor?

2 What force is pushing on the bench? What is its direction?

3 What can you say about the size of the forces that happen where the book touches the bench?

Measuring forces

The size of a force is measured in newtons. One **newton** is about the size of pull that you need to lift a small apple. You need a force of about five newtons to pick up a mug of tea. You would need a force of over 1000 newtons to pick up a Sumo wrestler!

You can measure the size of a force with a forcemeter. A forcemeter has a spring inside it. When the force is small the spring does not **stretch** much. When it measures a large force the spring is stretched more. Forcemeters have different ranges so that they can measure different sizes of force.

4 a What do we use to measure the size of a force?

   b What is inside this?

5 Look at the photograph. Which of the two forcemeters do you think will measure the larger force?

Forces between magnets

Two magnets produce a pair of forces whether they are touching or not. If you hold them one way, the magnets will produce a pair of forces that pull the magnets together. This is called **attraction**. If you turn one magnet round they will produce a pair of forces that push the magnets apart. This is called **repulsion**. There is a pair of forces that attract a magnet and a piece of iron or steel. One force acts on the magnet and one acts on the piece of iron or steel to pull them together.

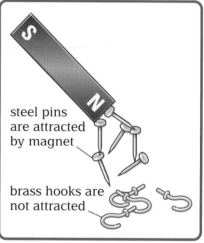

steel pins are attracted by magnet

brass hooks are not attracted

6 Look at the diagram of the fridge. Are the magnet and the fridge door attracting or repelling?

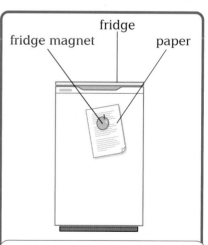

fridge magnet

fridge

paper

The fridge magnet does not attract paper. The fridge magnet and the fridge door attract each other through the paper

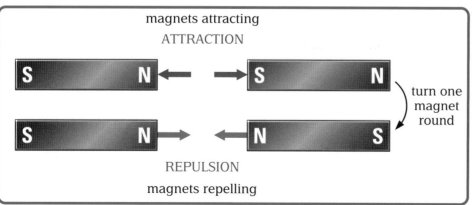

magnets attracting
ATTRACTION

turn one magnet round

REPULSION
magnets repelling

7 Draw a diagram showing the forces that act between the fridge magnet and the fridge. Use arrows to show forces.

7K.2 Weight

Some forces are very important. They have special names. One of these is the force we call weight.

The Earth pulls things towards it

When something is dropped it falls towards the centre of the Earth. This happens because there is a force on it called **weight**. The arrows in this diagram show the direction of this force on objects at different places around the Earth.

Weight is a force that happens whether or not the Earth and the object touch each other. You measure the weight of something when you hang it on a forcemeter.

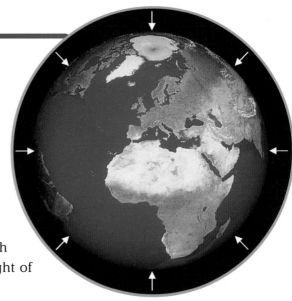

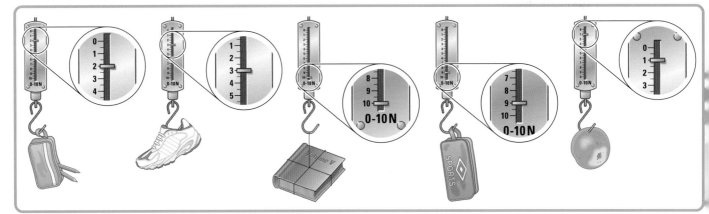

1 Write down the weights of the things shown in the diagram.

2 Which is the heaviest object shown?

3 If the sports bag was full of apples, about how many apples would it have inside it? (Assume the bag alone weighs 1 newton.)

Isaac Newton and gravity

In the 17th century Isaac Newton worked out that every **body** attracted every other body with a force he called **gravity**. (Scientists use the word 'body' when they talk about any object.)

The force of gravity is very weak. You only really notice it when one of the bodies is very heavy like the Earth or the Moon. The force of gravity between the Earth and a golf ball is about half a newton. This is big enough to notice because the Earth has a mass of about six million million million million kilograms. The force of gravity between two golf balls next to each other is so incredibly small it is not noticeable. It is about a two thousand millionth of a newton.

The attraction of gravity between the balls is too small to matter.

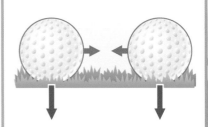

The pull of gravity from the Earth keeps the balls on the ground.

The idea of the force of gravity attracting everything is very important even if the force is very small for light objects. Newton used it to explain how all the planets and moons moved in the Solar System, how tides happened, what a comet was and many other things that people did not understand. His idea is still used today to plan space flights.

The pull of gravity from the Earth is what we call weight. The Moon is smaller than the Earth, so the pull of gravity on something on the Moon would be smaller than the pull of gravity on the same thing on the Earth. You weigh less on the Moon!

4 What is the name for the force that attracts every body to every other body?

5 Why don't you notice the force of gravity acting between two golf balls?

6 When do you notice the force of gravity?

Distance not to scale

The Earth's gravity is about six times bigger than the Moon's.

Weight and mass

Mass tells you how much stuff something is made of. Mass is measured in kilograms. Weight is the pull of gravity on the mass. The Earth pulls a 1 kilogram bag of sugar down with a force of about 10 N. If you had the same bag of sugar on the Moon it would still have a mass of 1 kilogram. However, because the gravity on the Moon is a lot less, its weight would be about 1.6 N.

The chart shows the weight of a 100 kg bag of sand in different places in the Universe. Remember that mass doesn't change even though the weight changes.

Location	On Earth	On the Moon	On Jupiter	In deep space	Near to a black hole
Mass	100 kg	100 kg	100 kg	100 kg	100 kg
Weight	1000 N	160 N	5400 N	Almost nothing	Too big to measure. Gravity is so big even light is pulled in. Nothing escapes a black hole!

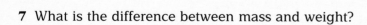

7 What is the difference between mass and weight?

8 What is the weight of a 3 kg bag of sugar on Earth?

9 Why is the weight of something on the Moon smaller than it is on the Earth?

10 Cookery books give the weights of things in grams and kilograms.

What is wrong with that?

7K.3 Stretching materials

When you pull on the end of a spring it gets longer. The size of the **extension** of the spring depends on the size of the force.

Measuring things that stretch

The diagram shows the apparatus you could use and the type of results you get when you do experiments to see how a spring stretches.

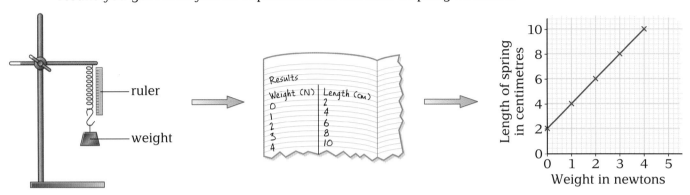

Look at the graph above. The spring is 4 cm long when the pulling force on it is 1 N. When you increase the pulling force by 1 N the spring gets 2 cm longer. This means that the extension goes up by 2 cm every time the pulling force increases by 1 N. If you use twice the size of force you get twice the size of extension. Three times the force gives three times the extension. We say the extension of the spring is **proportional** to the force. The graph is a straight line if this is true.

Sid and Eric perform some experiments for a spring and for a rubber band. Here are the graphs of their results.

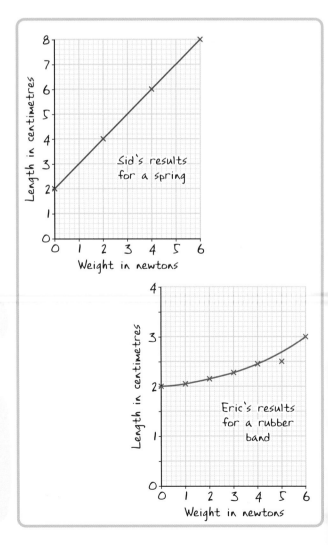

1. What force will make Sid's spring 5 cm long?

2. Do the spring and the rubber band follow the same pattern? Give a reason for your answer.

3. Which of Eric's readings looks like it was recorded wrongly? Give a reason for your answer. What should Eric do about the reading?

Different shape and thickness

Springs made from thicker wire need bigger forces to stretch them than springs made from thinner wire. This effect is used to make springs for forcemeters with different ranges.

Wire also stretches very slightly when you pull it. You have to use a much larger force to stretch a piece of straight wire than the force you need to stretch a spring. Stringed instruments use stretched wires to make musical notes.

The wire is usually called a string even though for many instruments the 'string' is actually a wire made from a metal like steel or from nylon. The string is stretched so it is tight enough to give the right note.

The top E string on an electric guitar needs a force of about 75 N to stretch it into tune. When it is stretched into tune it is about 7 mm longer than when it is slack. The total force on the tailpiece of an electric guitar when it is in tune is about 530 N! That is enough to pick up a 53 kg person.

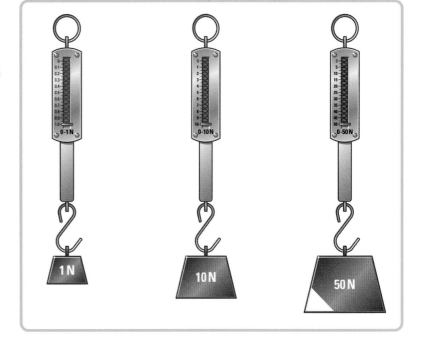

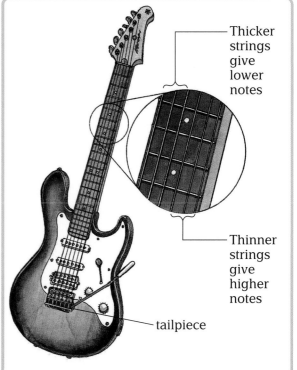

4 Which type of spring, one made from thick wire or one made from thin wire, needs the bigger force to stretch it?

5 Which substances are the 'strings' on musical instruments usually made from?

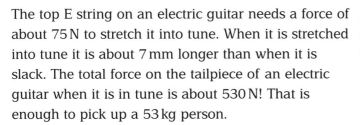

6 What type of spring, thick or thin, would you expect to find in a forcemeter with a range of 0 to 0.1 N? Give a reason for your answer.

7 Make a list of the places in a home where a spring, wire or elastic substance might be used because it stretches when a force is applied to it.

7K.4 Floating and sinking

Some objects float on water. This happens because a force is felt by an object in water.

Pushing water out of the way

When an object is put into a liquid it has to push some of the liquid out of the way. You can prove this by putting a golf ball into a beaker of water that is full to the brim. The water that is pushed out of the way flows over the rim of the beaker. You can see the effect if you put the same golf ball in a half full beaker with the level of the water marked on. This time the water that is pushed out of the way does not overflow, it moves to make the water level higher on the side of the beaker.

The liquid is pushed out of the way by the golf ball. There is a push up from the liquid on the golf ball. This upwards force is called **upthrust**. The picture shows how you can measure the size of the upthrust for a golf ball.

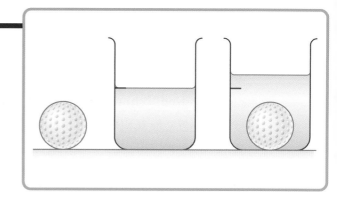

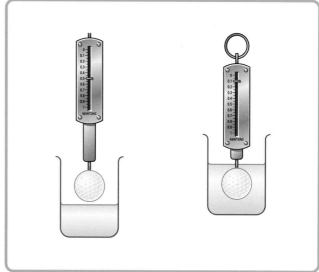

The upthrust depends on how much liquid is pushed out of the way. You can feel the size of the upthrust using a plastic lunchbox in a sink full of water. When you push it deeper into the water you can feel that the upthrust is bigger because more water is pushed out of the way.

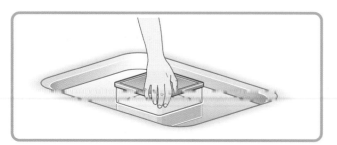

The upthrust is an upwards force from the water. Its effect is to cancel out some of the object's weight. The object seems to weigh less in water than it does in the air.

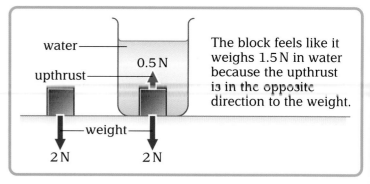

water —
upthrust — 0.5 N
weight
2 N   2 N

The block feels like it weighs 1.5 N in water because the upthrust is in the opposite direction to the weight.

1 When an object is put into water:

   a what happens to the height of the water?

   b what is the name for the force produced by the water?

   c what does the size of this force depend on?

Why some things float on water

Some things are light for their size. Lumps of cork, polystyrene ceiling tiles and sticks of balsa wood are examples of things that are light for their size. Blocks of steel, lead and concrete are heavy for their size. If something is light for its size it will float on water. This happens because the upthrust from the water is equal to the weight of the object.

The block of wood shown weighs 1 N. When it is put into water it pushes water out of the way. The upthrust increases as more water is pushed out of the way. When the upthrust is 1 N, the upthrust equals the weight of the wood. The wood floats.

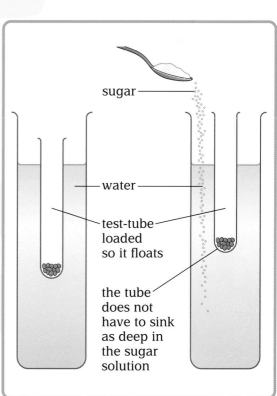

What happens when this mass is added?

Most of the wood needs to be under the water to create an upthrust equal to its weight.

2 What does an object have to do to the water to create an upthrust?

3 How big must the upthrust be for the object to float?

4 What do you think will happen to the block of wood if the 100 g mass is put onto the top of it?
(Hint: A 100 g mass has a weight of 1 N.)

Floating in heavier liquids

If the liquid is heavier than water then you do not need to push as much out of the way to get the same upthrust. You can make a liquid heavier by dissolving something in it. The water in the picture has been made heavier by dissolving sugar in it.

5 What has been dissolved in the water to make it heavier?

6 It is easier to float on a calm sea than it is on a calm fresh water lake. Suggest a reason for this.

sugar

water

test-tube
loaded
so it floats

the tube
does not
have to sink
as deep in
the sugar
solution

Comparing densities

You can use a number to describe how heavy something is for its size. This number is called the **density** of the substance. Density is actually a fair way of comparing the mass of different substances. To calculate density you need to know the mass in grams of one centimetre cubed of the substance. This can be calculated using this equation:

> density = mass ÷ **volume**

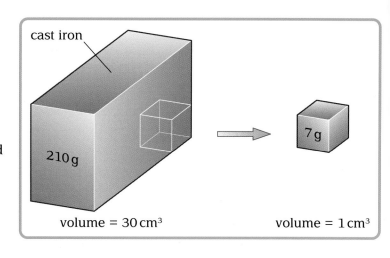

cast iron

210 g

volume = 30 cm³

7 g

volume = 1 cm³

For example, the block in the diagram has a mass of 210 grams and a volume of 30 centimetres cubed. Its density is

> 210 grams ÷ 30 centimetres cubed = 7 grams per centimetre cubed.

This means that if you cut 1 centimetre cubed out of it the mass would be 7 grams.

7 How do you work out a density?

8 What does the density tell you?

9 What would the density be for a block of metal with a mass of 350 grams and a volume of 50 centimetres cubed?

The density is a good way of telling if something will float or not.

Solid blocks of substances that float on a liquid have a density lower than the density of the liquid.

10 Look at the pictures. Describe how different materials behave in water and in olive oil.

11 Find out what a Plimsoll line is, who invented it and why.

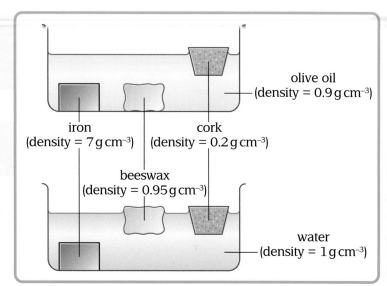

olive oil
(density = 0.9 g cm⁻³)

iron
(density = 7 g cm⁻³)

cork
(density = 0.2 g cm⁻³)

beeswax
(density = 0.95 g cm⁻³)

water
(density = 1 g cm⁻³)

7K.5 Friction

Friction is the name for a particular type of force. Friction is one of the most important forces in our lives. You couldn't walk without friction. Woven materials like clothes would fall apart without friction!

Places where friction happens

Friction happens when things try to slide past each other. It is a force you get when things touch. Friction forces occur when things are actually sliding and even before they start sliding. Look at the pictures of Eric and Sonja pushing the box.

1   Where does the friction force occur?
2   What is the direction of the friction force compared to the pushing force?

3   What happens to the box when the pushing force is bigger than the friction force?

Reducing friction

Friction is a problem when surfaces need to move over each other. Anything with moving parts has a problem with friction. Friction will wear away a surface where that surface meets another one. Friction also uses up energy. You can show this by rubbing your hands together. The friction soon warms them up! Movement energy is converted to heat energy through friction.

There are three main ways to reduce friction:

● you can make the surfaces smooth

● you can put a **lubricant** like oil on them

● you can design the moving parts so they roll on each other rather than slide.

You can judge how much friction there is between an object and a surface by tilting the surface. If the friction force is big, the object will not slide until the surface is quite steep.

Eric and Sonja push the box. It doesn't move.

A friction force balances the pushing force.

The friction force happens where the box touches the floor.

Eric and Sonja push harder. The box still doesn't move.

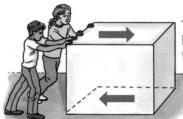

The friction force gets bigger. It still balances the pushing force.

The friction force is in the opposite direction to the push.

Eric and Sonja push harder still. Now the box moves.

movement

The friction force can't get any bigger. The pushing force is now bigger than the friction force. There is an unbalanced force. So the box moves.

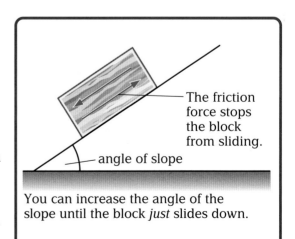

The friction force stops the block from sliding.

angle of slope

You can increase the angle of the slope until the block *just* slides down.

With a tin of beans standing on its flat end, the slope can get to 40° before the tin slides down. If you put the tin on its side, it rolls as soon as there is any slope at all.

about 40°

It takes a steep slope for the tin to slide.

about 3°

The tin rolls much more easily.

Rollers can be used to reduce friction when you are trying to move large blocks of stone. The same idea is used on a small scale in the wheels of a bike. The wheels of a bike turn on sets of ball bearings. These are designed to reduce friction because they roll rather than slide. You can also reduce the friction by using oil on the moving parts. We say that the oil <u>lubricates</u> the moving parts.

4 What does friction do to surfaces?

5 Name a substance that can be used as a lubricant.

6 What <u>three</u> things can you do to reduce the friction between surfaces?

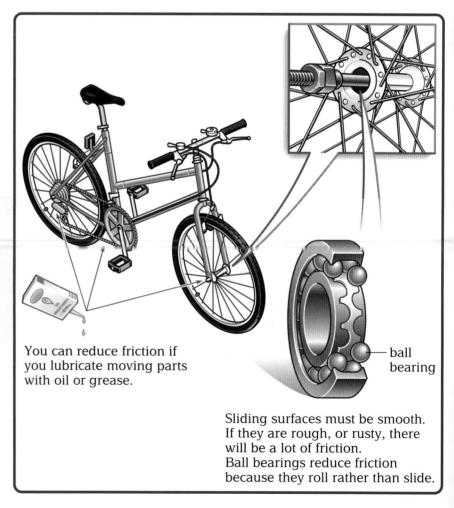

You can reduce friction if you lubricate moving parts with oil or grease.

ball bearing

Sliding surfaces must be smooth. If they are rough, or rusty, there will be a lot of friction.
Ball bearings reduce friction because they roll rather than slide.

Friction can be useful

If there were no friction you could not walk and your shoelaces would be impossible to tie. When you walk you push your foot backwards. The effect of the friction forces between your foot and the floor is to move you forward. This happens because the floor does not move. If you try the same thing off a skateboard, which can move, then you won't get very far because the skateboard moves back instead of you going forward. This happens because the wheels of the skateboard act like rollers and reduce the friction to a very low level.

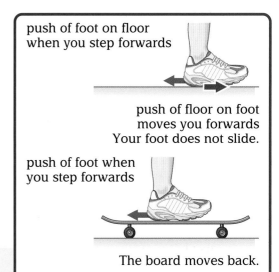

push of foot on floor when you step forwards

push of floor on foot moves you forwards
Your foot does not slide.

push of foot when you step forwards

The board moves back.

7 What is the effect of the friction force between your foot and the floor when you walk?

8 Why is it difficult to step forward off a skateboard?

9 Why is it difficult to walk on ice?

Another friction force

The friction force when something slides through air or a liquid is called **drag**. It slows things down and makes speeding up harder.

People who design racing cars spend a lot of time working out what shape the car has to be to make the drag as low as possible. The same idea is also used to design the shape of cars and vans so they do not use as much petrol. A car with a shape that moves through the air easily does not use as much petrol as a car of the same size going at the same speed with a shape that gives more drag. We say that the shape that goes through the air with less drag is more streamlined.

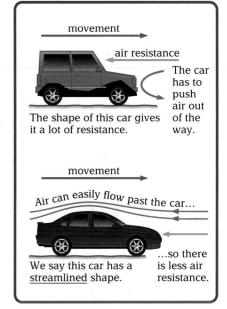

movement

air resistance

The shape of this car gives it a lot of resistance.

The car has to push air out of the way.

movement

Air can easily flow past the car...

We say this car has a <u>streamlined</u> shape.

...so there is less air resistance.

Drag can also be very useful. If you want to slow down the fall of an object you can increase the drag with a parachute. Some plants use the drag of the air to allow their seeds to be dispersed by the wind. The seed can travel a long way on the wind before it hits the ground. This means the new plant growing from the seed will not be competing with the original plant for food and space.

10 What is drag?

11 How can you reduce the drag on something moving through the air?

12 Describe some situations where drag is useful.

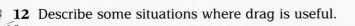

7K.6 Moving and stopping

Friction is used to stop things moving. Brakes and tyres are designed to make good use of friction.

Using the brakes

When you want to stop a bike or car you use the brakes. The brakes push on the wheels and produce a friction force. The friction force slows the wheels down. This is an example of where friction is useful.

Even if you have good brakes you need a good grip on the road as well. When you slow down the wheel, you produce a friction force between the road and the wheel that stops you moving forward. If your tyres do not have a good grip the friction force will be too small and you will skid.

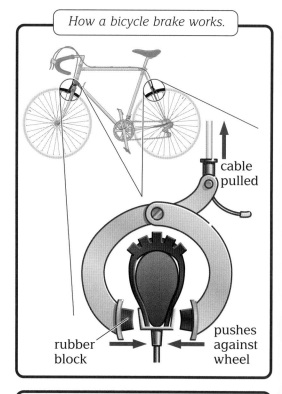

How a bicycle brake works.

cable pulled

rubber block

pushes against wheel

This tyre is old and very worn.

This tyre is brand new.

Did you know that a bald tyre actually grips a dry road better than a new tyre? But there is a problem when the road is slightly damp or wet. On wet or damp roads the bald tyre will slip all over the place and cause accidents. There is a law against driving around with bald tyres.

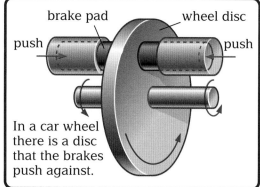

brake pad   wheel disc

push   push

In a car wheel there is a disc that the brakes push against.

1   What pushes on a wheel to slow down a bike or car?

2   When the wheel slows down what type of force is produced between the wheel and the road?

3   What might happen to a car that is slowing down if the friction force on the tyres is too small?

Speed and stopping

When you ride a bike or travel in a car you describe how fast you travel by the speed. **Speed** tells you how far you go in a certain time. A speed of 30 miles per hour (mph) means you would travel 30 miles in one hour if you kept

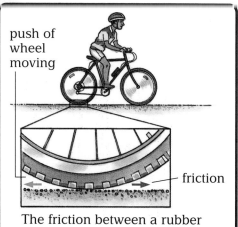

push of wheel moving

friction

The friction between a rubber tyre and a rough road surface moves the bike forwards.

going at that speed. A speed of 20 km/h means you would travel 20 kilometres in one hour if you kept going at that speed. The maximum speed that traffic is allowed to go at in built-up areas is 30 mph, which is about 48 km/h.

The speed of a car affects how long it takes to stop. The faster you are going, the longer it takes to stop.

The blue stripe shows the **distance** you travel while you are just thinking about stopping. If a driver is tired, affected by medicines, under the influence of alcohol or drugs, or even just distracted by a conversation with a passenger, the thinking distance can be a lot longer because reactions are slower.

The red stripe shows the distance you travel once you start to brake. If the road is slippery or the tyres are worn or if you start to skid then the braking distance will be a lot further.

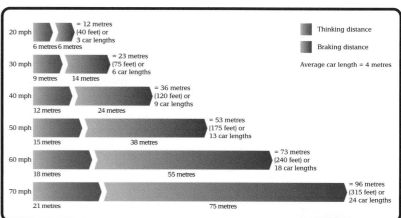

This chart is taken from the Highway Code.

4   What is the total stopping distance at 30 mph?

5   Why is the speed limit only 30 mph in built-up areas?

6   What type of things can make the total stopping distance for a car longer than those shown in the chart?

Showing a bike ride on a graph

If you plot a graph of the distance travelled against the time you take you get something called a <u>distance/time graph</u>. This type of graph gives you a picture of what is happening on the journey. A horizontal part of the line means you have stopped. A steep part of the line represents a high speed.

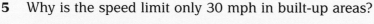

7   On which part of the journey is the speed of the cyclist the highest?

8   On which part of the journey is the speed of the cyclist zero?

9   Sketch a distance/time graph to show your journey to school.

You should now understand the key words and key ideas shown below.

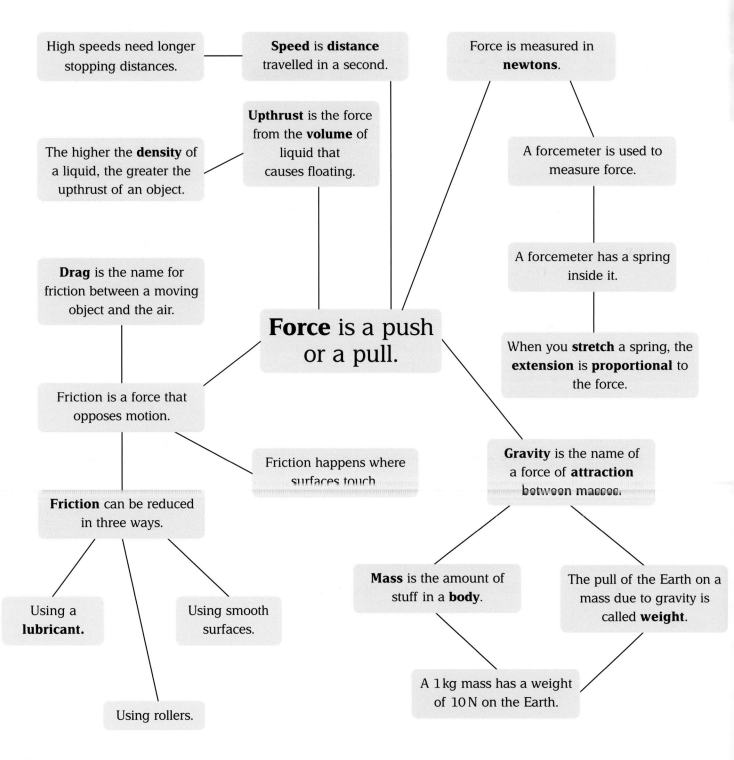

High speeds need longer stopping distances.

Speed is **distance** travelled in a second.

Force is measured in **newtons**.

Upthrust is the force from the **volume** of liquid that causes floating.

The higher the **density** of a liquid, the greater the upthrust of an object.

A forcemeter is used to measure force.

A forcemeter has a spring inside it.

Drag is the name for friction between a moving object and the air.

Force is a push or a pull.

When you **stretch** a spring, the **extension** is **proportional** to the force.

Friction is a force that opposes motion.

Friction happens where surfaces touch.

Gravity is the name of a force of **attraction** between masses.

Friction can be reduced in three ways.

Using a **lubricant.**

Using smooth surfaces.

Mass is the amount of stuff in a **body**.

The pull of the Earth on a mass due to gravity is called **weight**.

Using rollers.

A 1 kg mass has a weight of 10 N on the Earth.

The Solar System and beyond

In this unit we shall be studying the Earth and our neighbours in space, such as the Sun, the Moon and the planets. We will also consider our place in the wider Universe.

KEY WORDS
astronomer
axis
orbit
seasons
hemisphere
arc
body
star
solar
planet
satellite
lunar
phase
eclipse
Solar System
asteroid belt
galaxy
Universe
constellation

7L.1 The Earth in space

For thousands of years, people have wondered what causes day and night and the changing seasons. They have watched the Sun, Moon and stars move across the sky and they wondered if the Earth is moving too. Scientists who study these things are called **astronomers**.

Days like these

At dawn, we see the Sun rise in the East. It moves across the sky during the day and sets in the West. For many centuries most people thought this was because the Sun travels around the Earth.

Some people disagreed. In the sixteenth century a Polish monk called Nicolaus Copernicus realised that if the Sun stayed still and the Earth spun, we would see the same effect.

We say that the Earth spins on its **axis**. Imagine you had a giant cocktail stick and could push it right through the centre of the Earth from the North Pole, to the South Pole. This would show the line of the Earth's axis. It takes 24 hours for the Earth to make one complete turn on its axis. We call this a day.

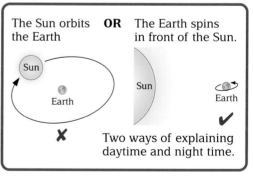

The Sun orbits the Earth **OR** The Earth spins in front of the Sun.

Two ways of explaining daytime and night time.

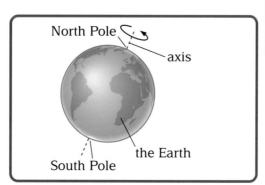

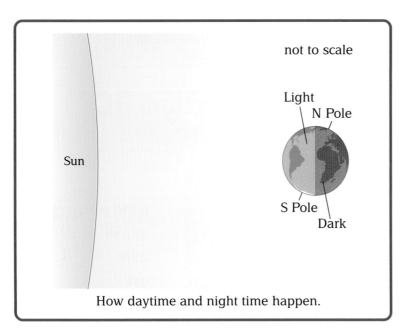

not to scale

Light
N Pole

Sun

S Pole
Dark

How daytime and night time happen.

Each star appears to move around the Pole Star.

Like the Sun and Moon, the stars seem to move across the sky. Only the Pole Star stays in the same place. This gives us further evidence that the Earth is spinning.

Only the parts of the Earth's surface facing the Sun are lit. On those parts it is daytime. The parts of the Earth's surface that are facing away from the Sun are in darkness; it is night time there.

The Earth never stands still. There are always parts of the Earth's surface that are moving into the light and other parts moving out of the light.

In the first picture the UK is facing the Sun and so it is daytime there. Australia is facing away from the Sun and it is night time there. India is just entering the dark side, so it is dusk.

12 hours later it is night time in the UK and daytime in Australia. In India it is getting light, so it is dawn.

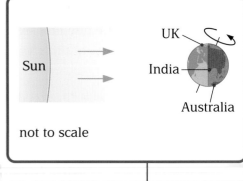

UK

Sun
India

Australia

not to scale

1 In which direction do we look to see the Sun rise?

2 How long does it take for the Earth to spin once on its axis?

3 If it is midday in the UK, what time do you think it might be in:

a India; **b** central Australia; **c** America's East coast?

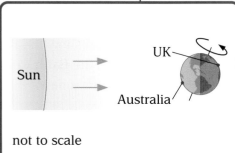

UK

Sun

Australia

not to scale

4 What are time zones? Find out how they are used.

Why we have years.

We know that the Earth spins. At the same time, the Earth travels around the Sun. We say that it **orbits** the Sun. We call the time it takes for the Earth to orbit the Sun a year.

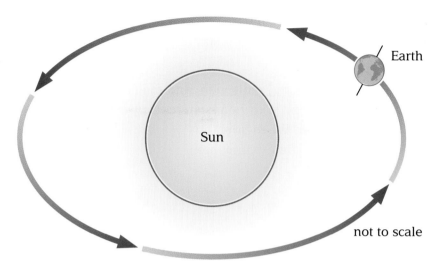

not to scale

The Earth takes a year to orbit the Sun.

During a year, the Earth makes $365\frac{1}{4}$ turns on its axis. So a year is really $365\frac{1}{4}$ days long! We can't have a $\frac{1}{4}$ day on our calendars so we round down to 365 days most years. Every fourth year, we catch up by adding a whole day. We call this a <u>leap year</u>.

5 How long is a year on Earth?

6 Explain why an Earth year is this length.

7 Why do we have leap years?

8 The orbit of the Earth around the Sun is not a perfect circle. It is a shape called an <u>ellipse</u>. Find out what an ellipse is and draw an elliptical orbit.

7L.2 The four seasons

As we go through a year, we notice the temperature changing. The number of hours of daylight in a day also changes. We can describe these changes by dividing the year into four **seasons**: spring, summer, autumn and winter.

We have seasons because the Earth's axis is tilted. This means that different parts of the Earth are tilted towards the Sun or away from it during the year.

We call the top half of the Earth the <u>northern hemisphere</u> and the bottom half the <u>southern hemisphere</u>. When your hemisphere is tilted towards the Sun, you are in summer. When your **hemisphere** is tilted away from the Sun, you are in winter.

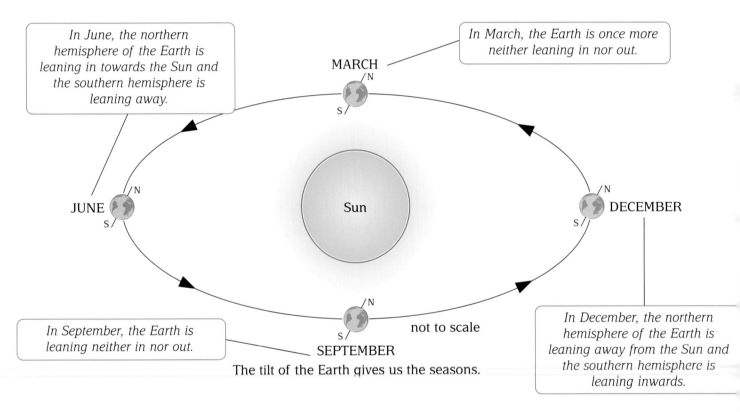

In June, the northern hemisphere of the Earth is leaning in towards the Sun and the southern hemisphere is leaning away.

In March, the Earth is once more neither leaning in nor out.

MARCH

JUNE

Sun

DECEMBER

In September, the Earth is leaning neither in nor out.

not to scale

SEPTEMBER

In December, the northern hemisphere of the Earth is leaning away from the Sun and the southern hemisphere is leaning inwards.

The tilt of the Earth gives us the seasons.

1 When it is summer in the UK, what season is it in Australia?

2 Name <u>five</u> countries in which it is summer at the same time as in the UK.

3 Find out where the Equator is. What do you think the seasons will be like there?

Why it is warmer in summer

One of the main differences between summer and winter is temperature. The tilt of the Earth's axis and the curve of the Earth's surface are the causes of this.

In summer, the rays of light from the Sun shine on a smaller surface area than they do in winter. This means that the rays are more concentrated and they have more effect. The part of the Earth that is tilted towards the Sun becomes warmer.

In winter, the Sun's rays are shining on a larger surface area than they do in summer. The Sun's rays are less concentrated, so the Earth's surface does not get so warm.

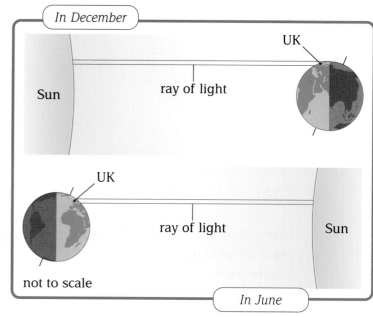

In December

Sun

ray of light

UK

UK

ray of light

Sun

not to scale

In June

4 Why is it warmer in summer than in winter?

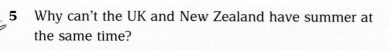

5 Why can't the UK and New Zealand have summer at the same time?

There is a second reason for summer being warmer than winter. In summer daytime lasts longer. This means that the Sun's rays have longer to heat the surface. This helps to raise the temperature.

Why we have more hours of daylight in summer

The second main difference between winter and summer is the length of daylight in a day. It takes 24 hours for the Earth to turn once on its axis, but night time and daytime are hardly ever equal.

The Earth's axis is at an angle to the line that divides daylight from night. In June the northern hemisphere spends more time in daylight than in darkness as it spins. It is summer there.

In December, the northern hemisphere spends less time in daylight than in darkness as it spins. It is winter there.

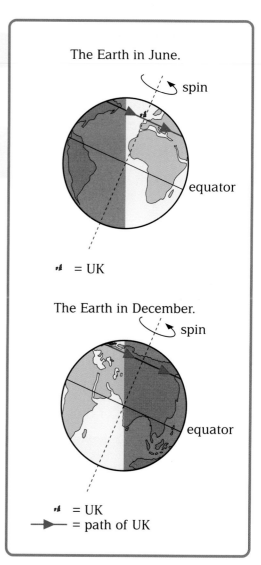

The Earth in June.

spin

equator

= UK

The Earth in December.

spin

equator

= UK
= path of UK

The part of the Earth which is in summer is tilted towards the Sun, so the Sun appears to be higher in the sky.

When the hours of daylight are long in summer, the Sun rises further back than East, towards Northeast. It then moves high into the sky, passing right overhead. It sets further round than West, towards Northwest. When the hours of daylight are short in winter, the Sun rises less far back, towards Southeast. It moves only a short distance up into the sky and sets only a little way round, towards Southwest. The shape of the Sun's path through the sky is called an **arc**.

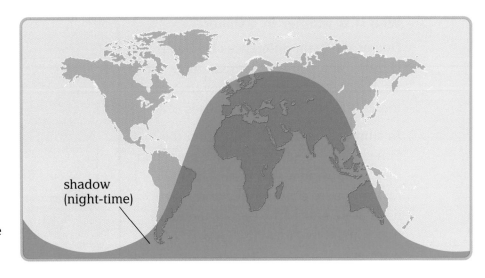

shadow (night-time)

6   Is the Sun's arc through the sky bigger in summer or winter?

7   In which month does the northern hemisphere have most hours of daylight?

8   In which month does the northern hemisphere have fewest hours of daylight?

9   In summer, how does the length of daylight on the Equator compare with the length of daylight in the UK?

7L.3   Lights in space

When you look up at the sky on a clear night away from street lights, you can see lots of dots of light.

- Some of these are stars.
- Some of these are planets.
- Some may even be manmade satellites in space.

Scientists who study this subject call the different objects in space **bodies**. We are going to explore how we see these bodies and consider the difference between them.

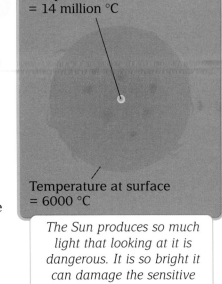

Temperature in centre = 14 million °C

Temperature at surface = 6000 °C

The Sun produces so much light that looking at it is dangerous. It is so bright it can damage the sensitive parts of your eye.

Stars

A **star** is a body that gives out its own light. We call this a <u>luminous</u> body. The nearest star to the Earth is the Sun. It looks bigger than all the other stars because it is much closer to the Earth than the others. Stars are like giant nuclear bombs that are exploding all the time. Things to do with the Sun are said to be **solar**.

Planets

Some stars have **planets** in orbit around them. There are nine planets orbiting the Sun. The Earth is one of them. Planets are giant lumps of rock or balls of gas. They do not give out their own light in the same way as stars do. We can only see these planets because they reflect the Sun's light. A planet is a <u>non-luminous</u> body.

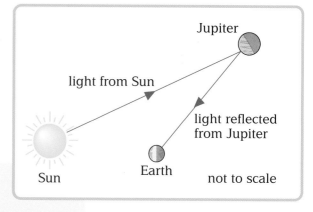

light from Sun

Jupiter

light reflected from Jupiter

Sun   Earth   not to scale

1 Why does the Sun look so much bigger than other stars?

2 Which types of body in space give out their own light?

3 Which types of body do not give out their own light but reflect it?

The Moon

The Moon is the closest body in space to the Earth. It orbits the Earth, so it is called a **satellite** of the Earth. Like the planets, the Moon does not give out its own light; it reflects light from the Sun. Things to do with the Moon are said to be **lunar**.

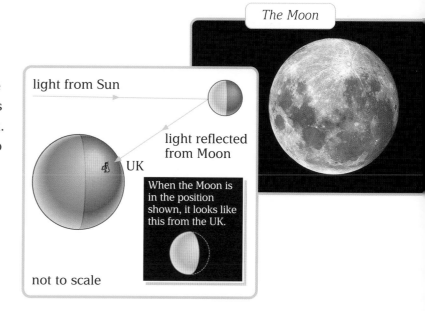

The Moon

light from Sun

light reflected from Moon

UK

When the Moon is in the position shown, it looks like this from the UK.

not to scale

Phases of the Moon

Just as with the Earth, half of the Moon is in sunlight and half is in darkness. We can only see the part of the Moon that is facing us and is reflecting the sunlight. The amount we can see varies, day by day.

The Moon takes 28 days to orbit the Earth. We call this a <u>lunar month</u>. The lunar month starts when we can see just a thin crescent of the Moon. We call this a New Moon.

As the Moon moves around the Earth, it shows us more of the side lit by the Sun. The crescent gets larger. We say it waxes.

When the light side of the Moon is completely facing us, we call it a Full Moon. It looks like a disc. If there are no clouds, a Full Moon can reflect enough light to see by.

The Moon continues to move and gradually less sunlight is reflected to us. The Moon becomes a crescent again as it wanes. At the end of the lunar month the side of the Moon that is in shadow is facing us. Light is not being reflected towards the Earth, and the Moon seems to disappear.

These stages that we see are known as the **phases** of the Moon.

4   What are the names given to bodies that orbit
    a a star?   **b** a planet?

5   How long does it take for the Moon to orbit the Earth?

6   If the Moon were a luminous body would we see it wax and wane?

7   Imagine you lived on the Moon. Would the Earth always look the same to you? Explain your answer.

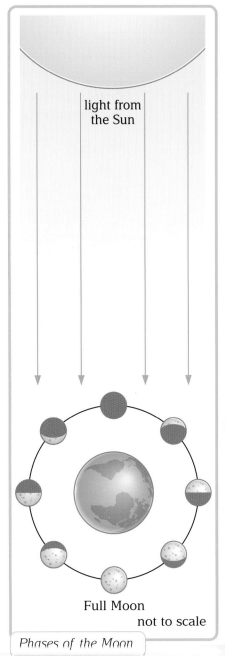

light from the Sun

Full Moon
not to scale

Phases of the Moon

7L.4 The Sun and the Moon

If we look at the Sun and the Moon from Earth, they appear to be about the same size. But this is just an illusion. The Sun is actually 400 times bigger than the Moon. If the Sun was the size of a house, the Moon would be the size of a mouse. However, the Sun is nearly 400 times further away from the Earth than the Moon is. The difference in their sizes is cancelled out by the difference in their distances from the Earth.

1   Is the Sun or the Moon bigger?

2   Is the Sun or the Moon closer to the Earth?

> *WARNING: Never look directly at the Sun (even with sunglasses on). You could damage your eyesight.*

the setting Sun

the Moon in exactly the same direction at a different time

The Sun and the Moon look the same size.

Solar eclipse

A solar **eclipse** occurs when the Moon passes between the Sun and the Earth so that the three bodies line up. The Moon casts a shadow on the surface of the Earth. The part of the Earth where the shadow falls will become dark, even though it is really daytime there!

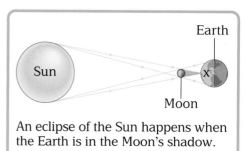

An eclipse of the Sun happens when the Earth is in the Moon's shadow.

x = total eclipse   not to scale

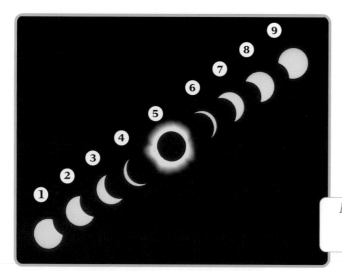

Nine photos of the stages of a total solar eclipse. Number 5 shows totality.

There was a total solar eclipse in August 1999. Across a large section of the world different countries came into the shadow of the Moon, and people were suddenly in complete darkness for just a few minutes. People near the edge of the shadow saw a partial eclipse. This is when the Moon doesn't block out the Sun completely.

3 What causes a solar eclipse?

4 What is the difference between a total eclipse and a partial eclipse?

You might think there should be an eclipse every lunar month. This is not what happens! The orbit of the Moon around the Earth is at a slight angle compared to the orbit of the Earth around the Sun. This means that the Earth, Moon and Sun do not line up very often.

5 When there is a total solar eclipse, the part of the Earth in the Moon's shadow becomes dark. Find out what else happens because of this sudden darkness.

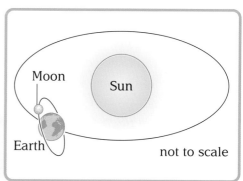

not to scale

Lunar eclipse

A lunar eclipse occurs when the Sun, Earth and Moon line up with the <u>Earth</u> in the middle. The Moon falls into the Earth's shadow. You would expect the Moon to completely disappear because there would be no light reaching it, but this is not quite what happens. The Earth's atmosphere bends some light from the Sun around to the Moon. This means that the Moon appears to be a red or orange colour. Again, because the Moon's orbit is at an angle to the Earth's orbit, lunar eclipses are much rarer than you might expect.

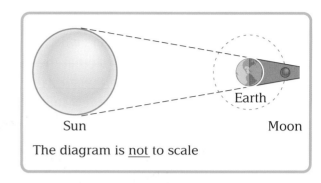

The diagram is <u>not</u> to scale

6 What causes a lunar eclipse?
7 Why does the Moon not disappear completely?

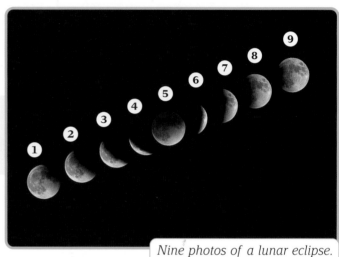

Nine photos of a lunar eclipse.

7L.5 The Solar System

Astronomers have discovered that there are nine planets orbiting the Sun. The Earth is one of them. We call this collection of Sun and planets the **Solar System**.

It took several centuries for astronomers to find all these planets. This was because we can't see some of them without telescopes. Early telescopes were not powerful enough to show us the most distant bodies in the Solar System.

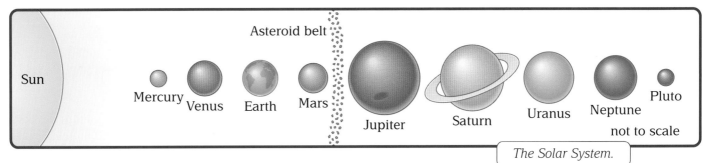

The Solar System.

Sometimes it is easier to remember a list if you can think of a saying with words that start with the same letters as the items in the list. This kind of saying is called a 'mnemonic'.

My	Very	Easy	Method	Just	Speeds	Up	Naming	Planets
Mercury	Venus	Earth	Mars	Jupiter	Saturn	Uranus	Neptune	Pluto

Astronomers find out a lot about the planets by studying their journeys round the Sun. We say they study the planets' motion.

Planet	Distance from Sun (million km)	Diameter of planet (km)	Time taken for one orbit (Earth years)	Time taken for one spin (Earth days)
Mercury	58	4800	0.25	59
Venus	107	12 200	0.65	243
Earth	149	12 800	1.0	1
Mars	228	6800	1.9	1
Jupiter	778	142 600	12	10 hours
Saturn	1427	120 200	29	10 hours
Uranus	2870	49 000	84	11 hours
Neptune	4497	50 000	165	16 hours
Pluto	5900	2287	248	6.5

Mercury, Venus, Earth and Mars are sometimes called the rocky planets because they have a surface that is made from rock. Jupiter, Saturn, Uranus and Neptune are large balls of gas and are called the gas giants. Astronomers are not sure whether Pluto is made from rock or from ice. There is also an **asteroid belt** orbiting the Sun between Mars and Jupiter. Asteroids are lumps of rock that are not big enough to count as planets. They might have come from a planet that broke up a long time ago.

1   Which planet is closest to the Sun?

2   Which is the biggest planet?

3   Which planet's day is the same length as Earth's day?

4   Which planet has the longest year?

Travel to the planets

Science fiction books and films often involve Martians (people from Mars) landing on the Earth. It's more likely that Earthlings will land on Mars. Small unmanned spaceships full of scientific equipment have already landed on the surface of Venus and Mars. We call these machines probes. A few people have walked on the Moon.

The surface of Mars.

5 Why do you think we know more about Venus and Mars than the other planets?

6 Pluto has a moon. Unlike the Earth's moon, Pluto's moon is nearly as big Pluto itself. Some astronomers think of this moon as our Solar System's tenth planet. Try to find out as much about the moon of Pluto as you can – including its name!

7L.6 Beyond the Solar System

Just as the Earth is one planet amongst nine in the Solar System, so the Sun is one star amongst millions. When we look into the night sky we can see some of them.

Where do stars go during daytime?

The Sun is so much closer to us than any other star that its light appears much brighter. It is so bright that we cannot see the light coming from the other stars. This doesn't mean that they are not there during the day. It is just that we cannot see them.

The Milky Way

A **galaxy** is a group of millions of stars. The Milky Way is our local galaxy. The whole Solar System orbits the centre of the Milky Way and it takes millions of years to complete one orbit. If you look into the night sky and see a band of stars across the middle of the sky, you are looking into the Milky Way.

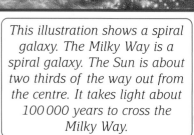

This illustration shows a spiral galaxy. The Milky Way is a spiral galaxy. The Sun is about two thirds of the way out from the centre. It takes light about 100 000 years to cross the Milky Way.

1 Why does the Sun appear to be so much brighter than the other stars?

2 What is the name of the galaxy that includes our Solar System?

3 Draw a sketch of our galaxy and show where our Solar System is.

The Universe

Just as the Sun is one of millions of stars in the Milky Way, the Milky Way is one of millions of galaxies that make up the **Universe**.

It is very difficult to imagine how big the Universe must be. The furthest any person has been from the Earth is to the Moon. That is 400 000 km away, but this is a very small distance compared with the distance to the edge of the Solar System. The next nearest star is 40 000 000 000 000 km away. Even this is a very small distance compared with the distance to the edge of just our galaxy.

Galaxies are spread out thinly with big spaces between them and they are moving away from each other at great speed.

There are millions of galaxies and millions of stars in each galaxy. Even if only some of these stars have planets orbiting them, there will still be billions of planets in the Universe. For life to exist on any of these planets the conditions need to be just right. Living things need an atmosphere to breathe, water and a suitable temperature. Could someone be watching you from another planet as you read this?

Constellations

Stars seem to make shapes and patterns in the sky. We call these patterns **constellations**. Some people believe that the stars control our personality and our fate. You may recognise names like Leo the Lion and the Plough.

If you follow the line of the two right-hand stars in the Plough you can find the Pole Star. The Pole Star shows you which way is North. People have used it for centuries to help them find their way.

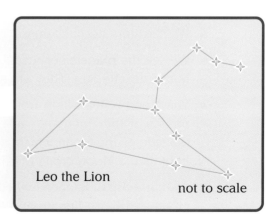

The Plough and the Pole Star.

4   How do the galaxies move in relation to each other?

5   Why is it useful to be able to find the Pole Star?

6   Why might sailors who navigated by the stars have difficulty if they sailed from the UK to Australia?

7   Name as many constellations as you can.

You should now understand the key words and key ideas shown below.

Key words

axis	arc	constellation
season	astronomer	orbit
eclipse	Universe	planet
hemisphere	star	asteroid belt
lunar	galaxy	body
satellite	Solar System	solar

Key ideas

- A day is the time that the Earth takes to spin once around its **axis**.

- A year is the time that the Earth takes to **orbit** once around the Sun.

- **Seasons** happen because the Earth is tilted on its axis. When the northern hemisphere is tilted towards the Sun, it is summer there.

- The days are longer in summer because the Sun's **arc** is bigger. This happens because of the tilt of the Earth's axis.

- We see stars because they are luminous.

- We see the planets because they reflect the light from the Sun. They are non-luminous.

- The Moon reflects light from the Sun; the phases of the Moon are caused by only seeing the side of the Moon which is in the Sun's light as the Moon orbits the Earth.

- A solar **eclipse** happens when the Sun, Moon and Earth line up and the Moon is in the middle.

- A lunar eclipse happens when the Sun, Moon and Earth line up and the Earth is in the middle.

- Nine **planets** have been found in the **Solar System**: Mercury, Venus, Earth, Mars, Jupiter, Saturn, Uranus, Neptune and Pluto.

- The nine planets orbit the Sun and these orbits take different times to complete.

- The Solar System is in a **galaxy** called the Milky Way.

- The Milky Way is one of many galaxies that make up the **Universe**.

- The Earth is the only planet that we know of that can support life.

- The stars appear to move across the night sky because the Earth is rotating.

Scientific investigations

Throughout Key Stage 3 you need to practise and improve your skills in investigations, just like you did at Key Stage 2. These pages and the activities that go with them are a reminder of the skills of:

- finding suitable questions for investigations;
- planning investigations;
- presenting results;
- coming to conclusions;
- evaluating the strength of evidence.

Finding suitable questions for investigations

When you do an investigation, you have a question to answer. Then you plan an investigation that you hope will give you the answer. But you can't answer all questions by doing a scientific investigation.

1 Look at parts **a** to **c**. Can you answer them by doing a scientific investigation? Explain your answers.

   a Is there a link between the height of a cat and the length of its whiskers?

   b Where is the rainiest place on Earth? (You can't visit everywhere on Earth, but lots of scientists have collected data about rainfall in lots of places.)

   c Are waterfalls beautiful? (Think about whether people agree on what is beautiful!)

Now think about the question of why elephants throw water over themselves. You can't answer it directly, but you can do an investigation using a model.

Elephants often spray water over themselves like this.

KEY WORDS
hypothesis
prediction
hazards
risk
risk assessment
scale
variable
vary
control
reliable
bar chart
line graph
conclusion
evaluation

First, you need to think of <u>ideas</u> that might explain why elephants throw water over themselves. We call these ideas **hypotheses**.

The idea that elephants do this to cool themselves is one that you can test. You probably haven't got an elephant, so you have to use a model! A plastic bottle full of hot water makes a suitable model. You can use a thermometer or a temperature probe and a data logger to show any temperature changes.

File Edit Object Type Tools View Help

The elephants are:
* just having a wash;
* trying to cool themselves;
* getting rid of parasites;
* chasing away flies;
* just playing.

2 Draw your idea of what the model elephant apparatus looks like.

3 Remember that you are trying to find out if water makes the elephants cooler.

   a Describe how to model throwing the water over the elephant.

   b What measurements will you need to write down?

Next, you need to say what you think your results will be. This is called making a **prediction**. You need to use the science that you know to give reasons for your prediction. Kirsty has made a prediction:

I think that when we pour cold water over the plastic bottle, the temperature of the water inside will fall.

4 Do you think that Kirsty's prediction is correct? Explain your answer as fully as you can. Remember that an explanation using scientific ideas will get you the best marks.

Planning investigations

When you plan an investigation, you need to think about:

- safety;
- the equipment and chemicals you will use;
- how to make your test fair;
- what to do.

Safety

Sometimes you need to use apparatus or chemicals that can be harmful. We call these things **hazards**. You can use them only if you make sure that you and other people are safe. You can look up some hazards in books and others on Hazcards, or you can ask your teacher for help.

Next you need to ask yourself how high a **risk** there is of the hazard causing harm. We call this a **risk assessment**. You do this to decide whether your investigation is safe enough to do. Sometimes the risk assessment helps you to see how to make your investigation safe, for example by wearing eye protection.

5 Where can you find out about possible hazards?

6 What must you do if you are not sure that your investigation is safe enough?

Selecting equipment

Some choices of equipment are easy. You need to be particularly careful when you choose measuring equipment. Instruments for measuring have a **scale** on them. You need to choose the instrument with a suitable scale for your particular investigation.

Sean is investigating the force needed to pick up objects in the lab. He estimates that the weight of these objects varies from 5N to 45N.

7 Choose the best forcemeter for Sean's investigation. Explain your choice.

Hazardous chemicals have warning labels. You need to be able to recognise them.

CORROSIVE

This is the sign for an irritant.

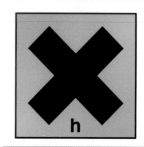

This is the sign for a harmful substance

Making your test fair

In an experiment, lots of things affect the results.
We call these **variables**.

To find out the effect of temperature on dissolving, you **vary** the temperature but keep the other things the same. We say that you **control** them. This is to make your test fair.

8 a Write down <u>two</u> things that you need to control or keep the same when you investigate the effect of temperature on dissolving.

b Why do you need to keep them the same?

9 If you vary the amount of stirring, what do you need to control or keep the same?

What to do

Before you do an experiment, you need to know exactly
- what you are going to do;
- what results you are going to record;
- how you are going to record your results, for example in a table on paper or a data logger.

You don't always get the same results when you do an experiment. To find out what is really happening, you have to:
- do your experiment several times;
- work out the average result.

You find the average by adding together your results and dividing by the number of results.

10 Why do you need to repeat an experiment several times?

11 Work out the average of these three numbers: 12.1, 12.3, 12.8.

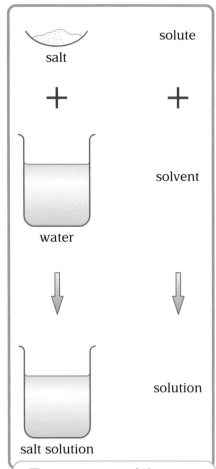

salt — solute

water — solvent

salt solution — solution

The temperature of the water, the size of the crystals and the amount of stirring all affect the time it takes for the salt to dissolve. These are all variables.

Geraint did an investigation to find out how long it took for different sized parachutes to fall to the ground. He worked out the average times for each parachute. This is sometimes called the **mean**. Here are his results.

Size of Canopy	Time Taken to Fall to the Ground (in seconds)			
	1st Attempt	2nd Attempt	3rd Attempt	4th Attempt
Big	12.25	12.45	13.23	12.64
Medium	9.53	11.37	11.14	10.68
Small	10.57	8.52	9.02	9.37

By repeating the readings Geraint has reduced any inaccuracies in the experiment so his results are more **reliable**.

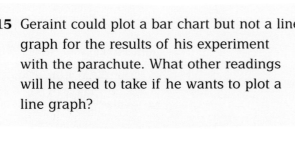

12 Look at Geraint's results. Write down <u>one</u> result that looks inaccurate.

13 Look at Geraint's average readings. Describe the pattern in these readings.

Presenting Results as bar charts or graphs

Sometimes it is difficult to see a pattern in a table of results. You can show results in other ways. For example, you can draw a **bar chart** or a **line graph**.

14 Draw a bar chart of Geraint's results.

Usually when you are plotting a bar chart or a line graph, the variable that you changed goes along the bottom (x-axis) and the one you measured goes up the side (y-axis).

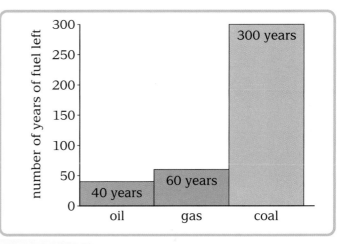

15 Geraint could plot a bar chart but not a line graph for the results of his experiment with the parachute. What other readings will he need to take if he wants to plot a line graph?

Coming to conclusions

The **conclusion** is where you say what you have found out, so it is an important part of your investigation. You need to describe the evidence that supports your conclusion. If you want to impress your teacher and get really good marks, you should try to use scientific ideas to explain why you got the results that you did.

This is Geraint's conclusion for his parachute investigation:

16 Which part of Geraint's conclusion:

   a decribes what he found out.

   b describes where he got the evidence to support his conclusion.

   c uses scientific ideas to explain why he got the results which he did.

> In my investigation I found out that when the canopy is bigger the parachute takes longer to fall to the ground. I know this because when I look at my bar chart I can see that as the size of the parachute increases the time it takes to fall increases as well. I think this is because a bigger canopy has a greater surface area so it catches more air as it falls. The bigger parachutes have more air resistance.

Evaluating evidence

The last part of any investigation is to consider whether there is enough evidence to support the conclusion. This is Geraint's **evaluation**:

17 What did Geraint think was wrong with his investigation?

18 Write down two ways that Geraint would improve his investigation.

19 What would you do to improve Geraint's investigation?

> I think my experiment was accurate because all of the points are on the line. However, I could have used more parachutes of different sizes to see if they fit the same pattern. If I did this investigation again, I would use three more parachutes. Also, if I measured the area of the parachutes and plotted the results in a line graph it would be easier to see any patterns.

Glossary/Index

Words in *italics* are themselves defined in the glossary.

A

acid a *solution* that reacts with many metals to produce a *salt* and *hydrogen*, and with *alkalis* to produce a salt and water   53–66, 69–70, 77

acid rain rain that is acidic because it has acidic oxides of sulphur and nitrogen *dissolved* in it   65

adaptation when plants or animals have characteristics which make them suitable for where they live   25–28, 30–33, 36

adolescent a person who is no longer a child, but is not yet an adult; a time of physical and emotional change   22–24

air a *mixture* of *gases*, mainly nitrogen and *oxygen*   70, 72–75, 81–82, 86–88

alkali a *solution* that reacts with an *acid* to produce a *salt* and water   55–59, 61–66

ammeter device used to measure *electric current*   122

amniotic fluid the *liquid* that surrounds and supports the *fetus* in the *uterus*   19, 24

ampere, amp, A *electric current* is measured in units called amperes   122

amphibian a *vertebrate* that lives on land and in water but has to lay its eggs in water   49, 52

anther part of a flower which makes the *pollen*   10

arc part of a circle   154

Aristotle (384–322 B.C.)   1, 46

arthropod an *invertebrate* with an outer skeleton with jointed legs   50–52

asteroid belt rock fragments orbiting the *Sun* between the *orbits* of *Mars* and *Jupiter*   159

attraction two objects pulling towards each other   135

B

axis an imaginary line through the centre of the *Earth* about which the *Earth* spins   149

battery two or more *cells* connected together   120,125

Bichat, Xavier (1771–1802)   1

biomass energy a *renewable energy* resource   113,115

bird a *vertebrate* with feathers   14, 46–47, 52

boiling point the temperature at which a *liquid* changes into a *gas*   85

brake a device which uses *friction* to stop a vehicle   146

Brown, Robert (1773–1858)   2, 81–83

Brownian motion *random* movement of *particles*   81–83

bulb a device which transforms *electrical energy* into *light energy*   119

Bunsen burner device which burns methane or propane to produce a hot flame   107, 108

Bunsen, Robert (1811–1899)   108

burning when substances react with *oxygen* and release energy; also called *combustion*   70–75

C

camouflage colouring to hide something against its background   27, 32

carbonate a compound that reacts with acids to produce carbon dioxide   69

carbon dioxide a gas in the air produced by animals and *combustion* or *burning* and when an *acid* *reacts* with a carbonate   19, 63–64, 69, 71, 73, 75

carnivore an animal that eats flesh   33–34, 43

cell (in biology) building block of plants and animals 1–2, 4–9, 12, 16, 23

cell (in physics) uses a chemical reaction to push *electric current* around an *electric circuit* 120,125,126

cell membrane the outer layer of the living part of a *cell* 6, 12

cell sap a *solution* of sugars and other substances found in the *vacuoles* of plant *cells* 6, 12

cell wall outer supporting layer of a plant *cell* 6, 9, 12

characteristics the special features of any plant or animal 37–38, 40–42, 44–52

chemical energy energy stored in *fuels* and food 106

chemical reaction a reaction between chemicals; it produces a new substance 67–69

chloroplasts tiny structures inside a plant *cell* which contain chlorophyll 6, 12

chromatogram the separated substances that are the result of *chromatography* 99–101

chromatography a way of separating a *mixture* of *dissolved solids* 99–101

cilia tiny beating hairs on the surface of some *cells* 7

ciliated epithelial cell a *cell* with tiny hairs called *cilia* e.g. found lining the windpipe 7

circuit symbols a shorthand way of drawing electrical *components* 120

classification sorting things into groups 46–48, 50, 52

climatic stress difficult environmental conditions caused by the climate 30, 36

coal a *fossil fuel* 109

combustion when substances react with *oxygen* and release energy; another word for *burning* 70

competition when several plants or animals are all trying to get the same things 35–36

components devices used in *electric circuits* 122

compress to squeeze into a smaller space 85

condensation when a *gas* cools and changes into a *liquid* 85, 97–98

conduction (i) the flow of an electric current through a substance

conduction (ii) in heat conduction, energy passes along a *solid* as its *particles* heat up and vibrate faster 89

conductor, of electricity will let electricity pass through it 119

conservation of mass a scientific law stating that no loss of mass happens in a chemical *reaction* 95

constellation a pattern of *stars* in the sky 161

consumer an animal that cannot make its own food, but eats plants and other animals 34, 36

Copernicus, Nicolaus (1473–1543) 149

corrosion the disappearance or change of substances such as metals when they *react* with chemicals such as water, *oxygen* or *acids* 68

corrosive substances substances such as *acids* and *alkalis* that *dissolve* or eat away other materials 54

crystal a substance that solidifies with a definite shape 81, 84, 93–94

crystallisation when crystals form from a melted or a *dissolved solid* 94

cytoplasm the contents of a *cell* excluding the *nucleus*; the place where most *chemical reactions* happen 6,12

D

dawn the time when that part of the *Earth* moves into the *Sun's* light 150

Democritus 79–81, 83

density the *mass* of unit volume of a substance 142

Desaulx   82–83

diffusion   the spreading out of a *gas* or a *dissolved* substance because its *particles* are moving at *random*   86

dilute   (i) a dilute *solution* is a weak solution containing very little *dissolved* substance   54

dilute   (ii) to dilute a *solution*, you add more *solvent*   54

disease   when some part of a plant or animal isn't working properly   20, 35, 54

dissolve   when the *particles* of a substance completely mix with the *particles* of a *liquid* to make a clear *solution*   55, 62, 65, 91–96, 99–103

distillation   *boiling* or *evaporating* a *liquid* and then *condensing* it to get a pure *liquid*   97–98

drag   the *friction* force acting on an object moving through air or water   145

dusk   the time when that part of the *Earth* moves out of the *Sun's* light into shadow   150

E

Earth   the third planet from the *Sun*   149,159

eclipse   when bodies line up in space casting one of those bodies into shadow   157

egg cell   female *sex cell*; also called an *ovum*   13–18, 23–24

Einstein, Albert   (1879–1955)   82–83

elastic potential energy   stored in things which are stretched or squashed   106

electric circuit   *components* connected together to allow *electric current* to flow   119

electric current   flows around a complete *electric circuit*   122

electrical energy   the energy in wires when *electric current* flows   106

element   a substance that can't be split into anything simpler by *chemical reactions*   71

embryo   a baby in the *uterus* before all its *organs* have started to *grow*   16–19, 22, 24

energy   energy is needed to make things happen   105

energy transfer   *energy* moving from one place to another   105

energy transformation   when *energy* changes from one type to another   105

environmental conditions   conditions such as light and temperature in the environment   25–27, 29–30, 36, 41

environmental variations   differences within a *species* caused by the environment   40–43, 52

evaporation   when a *liquid* changes into a *gas*   93–95, 97–98

evidence   observations and measurements on which *theories* are based   77–79, 81, 83

Exner, F.M.   82–83

expansion   when a substance gets bigger because its *particles* speed up and move further apart   88–89

explosion   sudden rapid *burning*   72

extension   the amount by which something gets longer   138

extract   a substance taken from or made from another substance; examples are the juices taken from plants that we use as *indicators*   57–58

F

fair test   a test in which one variable is changed and other variables are controlled or kept the same   11

family tree   a diagram to show how people are related to each other   40–41

fertile   able to *reproduce*   37, 52

fertilisation   when a male *sex cell* joins with a female *sex cell* to start a new plant or animal   10, 13–18, 24

fetus   a baby in the *uterus* whose *organs* are all growing   16, 19, 22, 24

inherited variations differences that parents pass on to offspring 40–42, 52

insect an *arthropod* with two pairs of legs and two pairs of wings 25, 28, 32, 44, 47, 51–2

insoluble a word to describe a substance that will not *dissolve* 92–93, 101–102

insulation material that does not conduct heat; it prevents heat loss 32

invertebrate an animal without a backbone 48, 50–52

J

Janssen, Hans and Zacharias 2

joule, J energy or *work* is measured in units called joules 105

Jupiter the fifth planet from the *Sun* 159

K

kilocalorie an alternative unit of *energy*, not used much anymore 117

kilogram, kg *mass* is measured in units called kilograms 137

kilojoule 1000 joules 116

kinetic energy *energy* in a moving object 106

L

Leap Year a *year* with an extra day; every fourth year 151

Leeuwenhoek, Antonie van (1632–1723) 2

light energy *energy* given out by luminous objects 106

lime-water a *solution* used to test for carbon dioxide; *carbon dioxide* turns the clear solution cloudy 69

liquid a substance that has a fixed volume but takes the shape of its container 67, 74, 80–81, 84–85, 88, 91–93, 97–98

litmus an *indicator* that is red in *acids* and blue in *alkalis*; it is *extracted* from a lichen 57–58

lubricant something, usually a liquid, that reduces the *friction* between moving parts 143,144

luminous gives out its own light 155

lunar to do with the moon 155

lungs *organs* for gas exchange between the blood and the air 7, 25, 70

M

mains electricity electricity supplied to our homes 130

mammal a *vertebrate* with fur and whose young develop inside the *uterus* 14–15, 21, 49, 52

mammary glands milk-producing glands; in the breasts in humans 21, 24

Mars the fourth planet from the *Sun* 159

mass the amount of stuff something is made of 137

melting when a *solid* heats up and changes into a *liquid* 85

menstrual cycle the monthly cycle in the human female reproductive system 18, 24

menstruation a monthly bleed in women when the lining of the *uterus* is lost; also called a *monthly period* 18, 24

Mercury the nearest planet to the *Sun* 159

micro-organism a microscopic living thing; some cause *disease* 21, 25

microscope an instrument for magnifying 1–6, 11–12, 15, 78, 81, 83

migration what animals do when they move to other places with the *seasons* 32, 36

Milky Way the name of our *galaxy* 160

mineral oil a *fossil fuel* 109

mixture a substance in which two or more substances are mixed but not joined together 91–93, 96, 99

model in the mind, it is a group of ideas and pictures 78

moon a natural *satellite* of a *planet*, usually a lump of rock   155

muscle cell a *cell* which contracts to cause movement   8–9

N

natural gas a *fossil fuel*   109

Neptune the eighth *planet* from the *Sun*   159

nerve cell a *cell* that carries nerve impulses   7

nerves carry electrical impulses around the body   132

neutral solution a solution that is neither *acidic* nor *alkaline*; it has a *pH* of 7   59, 61

neutralisation when an *acid* reacts with an *alkali* to make a *neutral solution* of a *salt* in water   61–65

Newton, Isaac (1642–1727)   136

newton, N *force* is measured in units called newtons   135

nocturnal active at night   28, 36

non-renewable a *fuel* which cannot be used again   110

northern hemisphere the part of the *Earth* north of the equator   152

nuclear radiation *energy* given out in nuclear reactions   111

nuclear reactors where nuclear fuel reacts to give *heat energy*   111

nucleus the part of a *cell* which controls what happens in the cell   2, 6, 9–13, 16–17

O

orbit the path of a *satellite* around a *planet*; the path of a *planet* around a *star*   149, 151

organ structure in a plant or animal made of several different *tissues*   1, 8, 12, 14–15, 19

ovary where *egg cells* (ova) are made   15, 24

oviduct the tube that carries an *egg cell* from an *ovary* to the *uterus*   15–16, 24

ovulation the release of an *ovum* from an *ovary* about once a month   15, 24

ovules contain the female *sex cells* of a flowering plant   10

ovum another word for an *egg cell*; the name for more than one is ova   18

oxide compound of oxygen and another element   70–71, 73

oxygen a gas in the air   8, 16, 19, 25, 70–73, 75

P

parallel circuit an *electric circuit* in which there are two or more different routes for the *electric current*   127

particle a very small piece of matter that everything is made of   79–89, 96, 99

particle model a way of picturing matter as made up of moving *particles*; also called the kinetic theory   83–89

penis male *organ* for putting *sperm* into the *vagina* and for passing urine   1, 15

period, monthly period the 'bleeding' when a woman loses the lining of her *uterus* about once a month; also called *menstruation*   18

petrol a *fuel* which can be burnt in a car engine   107

pH a scale, 0–14, that tells you how *acid* or *alkaline* a *solution* is   59, 60–65

phases of the Moon the different stages in the appearance of the *Moon* every lunar month   155–156

placenta the *organ* through which a *fetus* gets food and *oxygen* and gets rid of waste   19–20, 24

planet a body that *orbits* a *star*   154, 155

Pluto the ninth *planet* from the *Sun*   159

Pole Star the *star* directly above the *North Pole*   161

Pole, North the most northerly point of the *Earth's* axis   149

sodium chloride   common *salt*; a compound of sodium and chlorine   62, 94, 101–103

sodium hydroxide   a compound that *dissolves* in water to make an *alkali*   55–58, 60, 62–63, 94

solar cells   these transform *light energy* into *electrical energy*   114

solar energy   a *renewable energy* resource   112,114

solar panels   these transform *light energy* into *heat energy*   114

Solar System   the *Sun* and the nine *planets* in *orbit* around it   158

solid   a substance that stays a definite shape   67, 74, 80–81, 84–85, 88–89, 91, 93, 101–103

solubility   a measure of how *soluble* a substance is   101–103

soluble   able to *dissolve*   92–93, 99–102

solute   how we describe a substance that is *dissolved* in a *liquid*   92, 95–99, 102–103

solution   a *mixture* formed when a *solute* dissolves in a *solvent*   61–62, 91–99, 101

solvent   a *liquid* in which other substances will *dissolve*   92, 95–96, 98–100, 102–103

sound energy   *energy* given out by anything that makes a noise   106

southern hemisphere   the part of the *Earth* below the equator   152

species   we say that plants or animals which can interbreed belong to the same species   37–39, 42, 46, 49–52

speed   distance travelled in a certain time   146

sperm   male *sex cell*   13,15–17, 23–24

star   a body in space that gives out its own light   154,155

states of matter   *solids*, *liquids* and *gases* are the three states of matter   80–81

stigma   for a flower to be pollinated, *pollen* must land on this part   10

streamlined   designed to keep the *drag* to a minimum   145

Sun   the *star* at the centre of our *Solar System*   149

switch   used to break or complete an *electric circuit*   120

T

telescope   a device which magnifies objects in the distance   158

testes   where *sperm* (male *sex cells*) are made in animals; one is called a testis   1, 15, 23–24

theory   an idea to explain *evidence*   78–83

tidal energy   a *renewable energy* resource   112,114

tissue   a group of *cells* with the same shape and job   1, 7, 8, 12

turbine   this turns when you transfer *kinetic energy* to it from wind, water or steam   114

Tyndall, John   (1820–1893)   117

U

umbilical cord   contains the blood vessels that carry food, water, *oxygen* and waste between the *placenta* and the *fetus*   19–20, 24

universal indicator   an *indicator* that has many different colours depending on the *pH* of the *solution* that it is in   59–61

Universe   a group of billions of *galaxies*   161

upthrust   upwards *force* on an object in a *liquid*   140

Uranus   the seventh *planet* from the *Sun*   159

uterus   the *organ* where a baby develops before birth   14–16, 18–20, 24

V

vacuole   space filled with *cell sap* in the *cytoplasm* of a plant *cell*   6, 12

vagina   opening of human female reproductive system   15, 20

variable resistor   a *resistor* whose value can be changed   124

variations, vary   differences between members of a species   29, 37–42, 52

Venus   the second *planet* from the *Sun*   159

vertebrate   an animal with a skeleton made of bone inside its body   48–49, 52

Virchow, Rudolf   (1821–1902)   9

volt, V   *voltage* is measured in units called volts   125

Volta, Alessandro   (1818–1889)   132

voltage   a measure of the amount of *energy* supplied to an *electric circuit*   125

W

wave energy   a *renewable energy* resource   112, 115

weight   the force of *gravity* on a *mass*   136

wind energy   a *renewable energy* resource   112,114

word equation   a way of writing down what happens in a chemical reaction   68, 70–73

work   change in *energy*   105

Y

year   the time for a *planet* to complete one *orbit* of the *Sun*   151

Acknowledgements

We are grateful to the following for permission to reproduce photographs.

John Adds 4b, 5cl, 5cr; **B & C Alexander** 14l; **Art Directors and Trip** 2l (M Walker), 4t (M Walker), 4b (M Walker), 5r (M Walker), 13l (M Walker), 17b (M Walker), 20br (M Walker), 28c (M Walker), 38t (M Walker), 38bl (M Walker), 38m (M Walker), 49bl (Warren Jacobs), 70, 71tl, 71cl, 71bl, 73t, 73r, 73cl, 73cr; **Bubbles Photolibrary** 20t, 116l (Jennie Woodcock), 116tr (Angela Hampton), 116br (Chris Rout); **Bruce Coleman Collection** 26l, 26r, 28bl, 28tr, 32; **Corbis** 72t,72b (Bettman), 74 (James Corwin); **Ida Cook** 55r, 67 (all), 102; **Greg Evans Picture Library** 38cl, 38cr, 38r; **Mary Evans Picture Library** 40; **Mark Farrell** 62; **Philip Harris Education** 97, 135; **Andrew Lambert** 64b, 69, 71br; **Microscopix** 2t (Andrew Syred); **Vanessa Miles** 94, 146; **National Motor Museum** 73br; **Natural History Photolibrary** 109 (Daniel Heuclin); **Nature Picture Library** 136 (Tony Heald); **Natural History Photographic Agency** 27 (Michael Tweedie), 28br (Stephen Dalton); **Oxford Scientific Films** 2r, 6t (Kent Wood), 6b, 14t (Michael Fogden), 49tl, 49tc, 49tr, 49br, 50; **Science and Society** 110 (NMPFT); **Science Photo Library** 1, 5l (Claude Nurilsang & Marc Perenou), 5r, 13r, 16 (C C Studios), 17t, 20 bl, 21, 39 (Peter Menzel), 46, 64t (Prof. P Motta), 70l (CNRI), 70r (D Philips), 71tr (Martin Bond), 71cr (Jerry Mason), 79 (SPL), 81t (Northwestern University Library), 81b (SPL), 84 (Martin Dohrn), 105l (David Ducros), 105c (Jim Selby), 105tr (Alan and Sandy Carey), 105br (Simon Fraser), 107 (l-r) (Deep Light Productions, David Nunuk, Alan Sirulnikoff, Martin Bond), 111 (Mark Clarke), 116c (Simon Fraser), 117 (David Frazier/Agstock), 136 (Hank Morgan/Geosphere Project), 150 (Pekka Parviainen), 155 (John Sandford), 157 (Dr Fred Espenak), 158t (Dr Fred Espenak), 158c (David Nanuk), 158b (New York Public Library), 160t (NASA), 160b (Julian Baum), 161 (SPL); **Still Pictures** 65 (Mark Edwards); **Wellcome Trust Medical Photographic Library** 3t, 55c; **Janine Wiedel** 37

Picture research: Vanessa Miles and Jacqui Rivers

The publisher has made every effort to trace copyright holders, but if they have inadvertently overlooked any they will be pleased to make the necessary arrangements at the earliest opportunity.